PAUL

THE APOSTLE OF THE GENTILES

--- ✳ ---

JOURNEYS IN GREECE

EDITIONS HAITALIS

PAUL

THE APOSTLE OF THE GENTILES

———— ✳ ————

FIRST EDITION
January 2003

Editing and DTP: Barrage Ltd

Texts: Maria Mavromataki

Art Editing: Fotini Svarna

Colour seperations: Haitalis

Printing: Lithografiki S.A.

Photographs: Haitalis Publishing Co. archive

Published by: HAITALIS
13, ASTROUS ST., 13121 ATHENS,
GREECE
Tel: 210 5766.883
Fax: 210 5729.985

CONTENTS

INTRODUCTION 8

PAUL BEFORE
HIS CONVERSION 13

THE VISION ON
THE DAMASCUS ROAD 16

THE PREACHING OF PAUL 21

THE APOSTLE
OF THE GENTILES 28

THE FIRST JOURNEY:
CYPRUS 34

SECOND JOURNEY
THE VISION AT TROAS 44

ARRIVAL IN GREECE
SAMOTHRACE - KAVALA 49

PHILIPPI 54

AMPHIPOLIS - APOLLONIA 67

THESSALONIKI 70

VERIA (BEREA) 83

DION 86

ATHENS 88

CORINTH 106

THIRD JOURNEY 122

MYTILENE CHIOS - SAMOS ... 124

COS - RHODES 130

CRETE 135

THE END OF PAUL 140

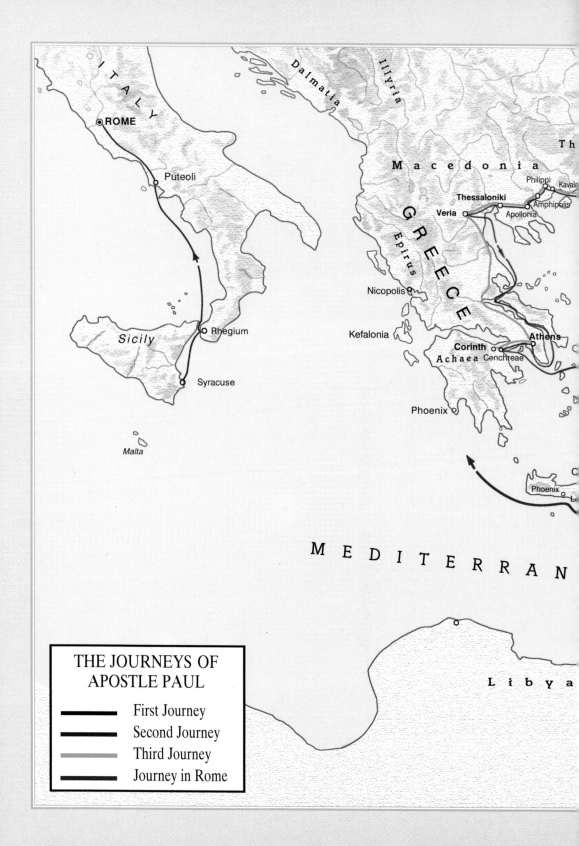

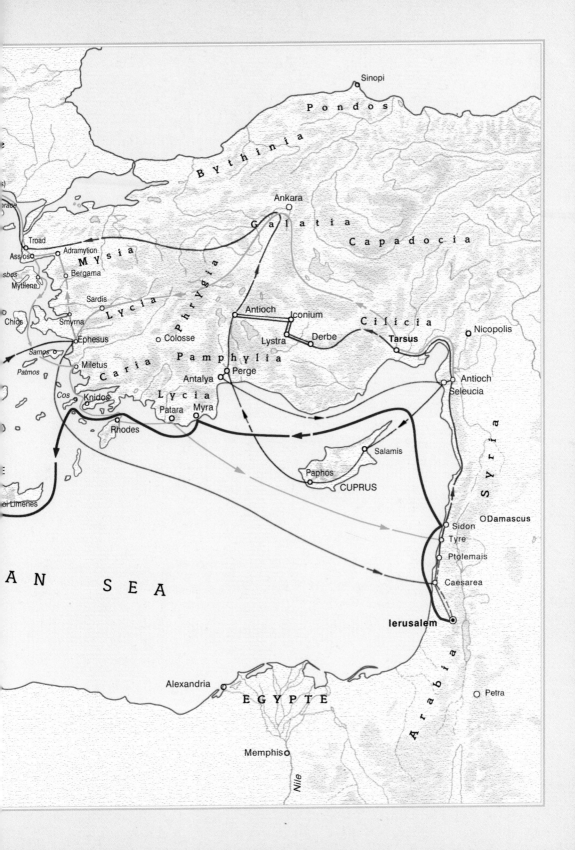

"He who was constantly concerned for the whole world, for its nations and its cities, but also individually for each and every one, with what could he be compared? With what precious metal or with what diamond? What could that soul be called? Gold or diamond? It was more adamantine than any diamond and more precious than gold and precious stones. Superior in strength and endurance, superior in value. With what substance, then, shall we compare him? With none that exists.

If diamond became gold and gold diamond, then we should be able to give an image of the soul of Paul. But why compare him with diamond and gold? Put the whole world on one side of the scale and you will see that the soul of Paul outweighs it.

...And if the world is not worthy of him, who then is worthy? The heavens? Before him, even they are small..."

St JOHN CHRYSOSTOM

Apostle Paul, icon in the Byzantine and Christian Museum

INTRODUCTION

"You will receive power when the Holy Spirit comes upon; and you will bear witness for me in Jerusalem and throughout all Judaea and Samaria and even to the farthest corners of the earth" (Acts 1, 8).

This was the last message which Jesus Christ addressed to His disciples when He appeared to them in Jerusalem after the Resurrection. When He had been received into the heavens, the fiery tongues of the Holy Spirit transformed the Apostles from illiterate fishermen into enlightened preachers of the Word of God. Through their ceaseless labours in spreading the Gospel, the first Christian communities gradually took shape in Jerusalem and Samaria.

If the disciples of Christ opened up the road to Christianity, it was the Apostle Paul who laid the foundations of the new religion. Once a fanatical persecutor of the Christians, he soon embraced their message and devoted the rest of his life to his so-called missionary journeys. In a series of journeys throughout the Mediterranean basin he succeeded in carrying the Christian message outside the borders of Judaea, from Asia Minor and Greece to Italy and Spain. The handing on of the new religious ideas to Europe was almost exclusively due to St Paul.

The missionary activities of Paul, his thinking and his teaching are recorded in detail in Holy Scripture. Thirteen of the epistles which are included in the New Testament canon are ascribed to him. "This greeting is in my own handwriting; all genuine letters of mine bear the same signature - Paul" (II Thess. 3, 17). Whether written by himself or dictated to one of his companions, the epistles of Paul constitute the most basic source of information on his activities. These are actually treatises on issues arising from Christianity, addressed to Christians or to Christian churches. Particularly informative on his travels in Greece are the epis-

9. Jesus Christ and the Apostles (the Vine), icon in the Byzantine and Christian Museum

tles to the Greek cities of Corinth, Philippi and Thessaloniki, which are at the same time the earliest examples of Christian literature.

Paul's letters appear to have been composed around the middle of the first century AD; it was some decades later that Luke wrote the Acts of the Apostles as a continuation of his Gospel. In the Acts, Luke gives an account of the founding of the earliest church and of the deeds of the apostles, with particular emphasis on those of the Apostle of the Gentiles, Paul. As his physician and companion on his journeys, Luke describes the course of Paul's life and labours from Damascus to Rome, drawing upon the testimony of eyewitnesses, as well as his own personal experience. The Acts of the Apostles is now considered a trustworthy historical source and serves as an illuminating introduction to Paul's epistles.

Nevertheless, none of these works provides adequate information either about Paul's early years or about the end of his life. This gap is filled by the First Epistle of Clement, to the Corinthians, which was written at the end of the first or the beginning of the second century AD. According to Clement, Paul was imprisoned seven times and subjected to stoning; he travelled to the West and was put to death, confessing his faith.

St Paul has been described by some commentators as Christianity's second founder, after Christ Himself. We have no means of knowing whether in his youth he had actually met Jesus, but after his conversion his soul was dominated by the belief that Christ Himself had taken pity on him and granted him His grace. The whole of his labours were based on the unshakeable conviction that he had been commissioned by God to achieve a great objective. His love for Christ and his natural inclination to fight to the end for his principles and ideals were the factors which ensured the success of his endeavours. These were his weapons in the face of danger, the hardships of his journeys, deprivations and persecution. " ... scourged ... many a time face to face with death. Five times the Jews have given me the thirty-nine strokes; three times I have been beaten with rods; once I was stoned; three times I have been shipwrecked, and twenty-four hours I was adrift on the open sea. I have been constantly on the road; I have met dangers from rivers, dangers from robbers, dangers from my fellow-countrymen, dangers from foreigners, dangers in the town, dangers in the wilderness, dangers at sea, dangers from false Christians. I have toiled and drudged and often gone without sleep; I have been hungry and thirsty and have often gone without food; I have suffered from cold and exposure. Apart from the external things, there is the responsibility that weighs on me every day, my anxious concern for all the churches. Is anyone weak? I share his weakness. If anyone brings about the downfall of another, does my heart not burn with anger? If boasting there must be, I will boast of the things which show up my weakness. He who is blessed for ever, the God and Father of the Lord Jesus, knows that what I say is true" (II Cor. 11, 23 - 31).

When Paul wrote these words he still had to come greater sufferings: imprisonment and death. Whilst he was a prisoner in Rome, a little before the end, his courage was still unshaken and he was ready to sacrifice himself. "As for me, my life is already being poured out on the altar, and the hour of my departure is upon. I have run the great race, I have finished the course, I have kept the faith. And now there awaits me the garland of righteousness which the Lord, the righteous Judge, will award to me on the great day, and not to me alone, but to all who have set their hearts on His coming appearance" (II Tim. 4, 6 - 8)

11. Apostle John, detail from the mosaic of the Crucifixion in the Monastery of Daphni, about 1100 AD

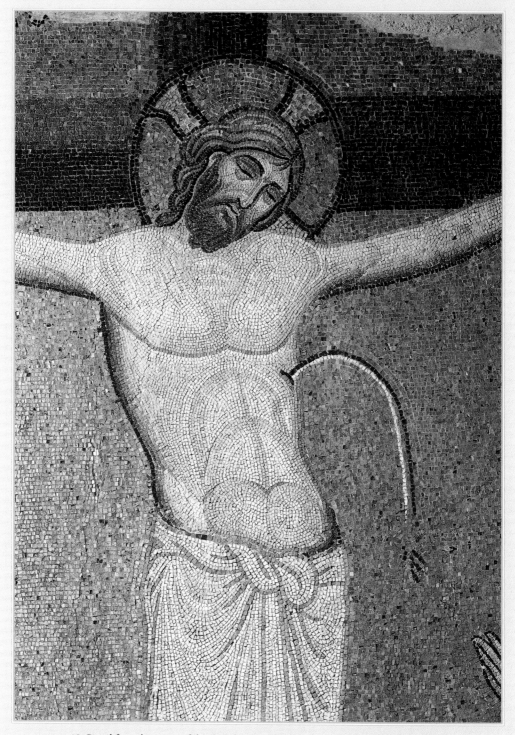

12. Detail from the mosaic of the Crucifixion in the Monastery of Daphni, about 1100 AD

PAUL
BEFORE HIS
CONVERSION

P aul, known by his Jewish name of Saul, was born at Tarsus in Cilicia in the early first century AD. Although his exact date of birth cannot be traced, we know that at the time of the stoning of the first Christian martyr, Stephen, in 33 or 34 AD, he was young: "They ... threw him out of the city, and set about stoning him. The witnesses laid their coats at the feet of a young man named Saul" (Acts 7, 58). Important information about his origins is given very frequently in the epistles: " ... Israelite by race, of the tribe of Benjamin, a Hebrew born and bred; in my practice of the law a Pharisee" (Phil. 3, 5). He was also a Roman citizen, while in his native city he had come into contact with Greek culture at an early stage.

Tarsus, one of the most important cities in the Roman province of Cilicia, was particularly prosperous through commerce and was a centre of culture. Paul himself took pride in this fact: "I am ... a Jew from Tarsus in Cilicia, a citizen of no mean city" (Acts 21, 39). In Tarsus Judaism had encountered and co-existed harmoniously with the Graeco-Roman tradition. The city's school of philosophy rivalled that of Athens or Alexandria, and was the headquarters of famous Stoic philosophers of the time. Greek must have been taught in its schools, since Paul knew the language and handled it skillfully and forcefully. It was in Greek that he wrote almost all his letters, while he studied the Scriptures in the Greek translation of the Septuagint, made in Alexandria in the third century BC. Paul was, of course, a polyglot and this advantage was of decisive importance for his missionary work. "Thank God, I am more gifted in tongues than any of you" (I Cor. 14, 18). His knowledge of languages was the tool of his teaching, the means of spreading the Christian message.

Through the language of the Greeks he encountered their culture. Certain passages in the epistles presuppose some knowledge, direct or indirect, of the Greek poets, such as the phrase "Bad company ruins good character" (I Cor. 15, 33), which is to be found in Euripides and Menander. Moreover, the use of specific philosophical terms, images and ideas is evidence of a certain familiarity with the Greek way of looking at the world. Nevertheless, the basis of his thinking was purely Jewish and no Greek influences had succeeded in contaminating the well-springs of his origin. It was only when Paul embraced Christianity that he reconciled Judaism and Hellenism in a new language, that of Jesus Christ.

His study of Jewish theology was begun in the synagogue at Tarsus and completed in Jerusalem. As he himself tells us: " ... a native of Tarsus in Cilicia. I was brought up in this city, and as a pupil of Gamaliel I was thoroughly trained in every point of our ancestral law. I have always been ardent in God's service ..." (Acts 22, 3). Gamaliel was a leading teacher of the law, known for his prudence and moderation. A good time before Paul's conversion, he defended the apostles from the death sentence which the Jewish chief priests wished to pass on them. With

Gamaliel, Paul immersed himself in the Jewish Law, with the intention of becoming a rabbi. The profound knowledge which he thus acquired is apparent in the ease with which he quotes large numbers of Old Testament passages in his letters. Moreover, the line of argumentation which he used to win over Jews to Christianity was drawn from the Scriptures themselves. Almost all the Epistle to the Hebrews, in which Paul attempts to demonstrate the superseding by Christ and the new faith of all the prophets, the Law and the religion of form of the Jews, is based on the Old Testament.

Nonetheless, before Paul accepted the Christian teaching, it was this very knowledge of the Jewish Law which was the principal weapon in the fight against Christianity. The hostility of the Jews towards the followers of Christ was inevitable, since it was upon the correct implementation of the Law that Israel made its future, its liberation from Rome and the fulfilment of the prophecies of its glory among the nations dependent. In these circumstances - but also because of his strength of personality - Paul soon became an enemy of

15. Jesus Christ, mosaic from the Monastery of Hosios (Blessed) Lukas, about 1030-1040 AD

17. Detail from the wall-painting of the Crucifixion in the Church of Perivleptos at Mystras, 1360-1370 AD

Christianity. "You have heard what my manner of life was when I was still a practising Jew: how savagely I persecuted the church of God and tried to destroy it; and how in the practice of our national religion I outstripped most of my Jewish contemporaries by my boundless devotion to the traditions of my ancestors" (Gal. 1, 13 - 14).

This hostility found active expression for the first time at the stoning of Stephen. According to the Acts of the Apostles, when Christ appeared to Paul, he showed himself penitent for his part in Stephen's martyrdom: " ... when the blood of Stephen, your witness, was shed, I stood by, approving, and I looked after the clothes of those who killed him" (Acts 22, 20). From that time on, until his conversion, the fight against the Christians became the sole purpose of his life. "Saul, meanwhile, was harrying the church; he entered house after house, seizing men and women and sending them to prison" (Acts 8, 3). When the Gospel spread as far as Samaria and the Christian community grew in numbers, Saul's persecuting zeal became even more merciless.

Christianity was for him a dire heresy which was undermining the Jewish religion and betraying the word of God. "I myself once though it my duty to work actively against the name of Jesus of Nazareth; and I did so at Jerusalem. By authority obtained from the chief priests, I sent many of God's people to prison, and when they were condemned to death, my vote was cast against them. In all the synagogues I tried by repeated punishment to make them commit blasphemy; indeed my fury rose to such a pitch that I extended my persecution to foreign cities" (Acts 26, 9 - 11).

In pursuit of these tactics, he decided to go to Damascus. In the meantime, he had received written permission from the high priest to arrest the Christians in those parts and to take them to Jerusalem (Acts 9, 2). However, his plans for Damascus were never carried out, because, as he himself relates: "It was by a revelation that his secret purpose was made known to me ... In former generations that secret was not disclosed to mankind ... Such is the gospel of which I was made a minister by God's unmerited gift, so powerfully at work in me. To me, who am less than the least of all God's people, He has granted the privilege of proclaiming to the Gentiles the good news of the unfathomable riches of Christ ... (Eph. 3, 3 - 8).

THE VISION ON THE DAMASCUS ROAD

The conversion of Paul to Christianity was a unique event which altered the course of history for the whole of humanity. The Apostle of the Gentiles makes frequent references in his epistles to the miraculous way in which Christ appeared before him on the road to Damascus. However, a detailed account of the event is to be found in the Acts of the Apostles - no fewer than three times (Chapters 9, 22 and 26). The three narratives complement one another, while the fact that they were written by someone who was a companion of Paul renders them all the more authoritative.

All the accounts which we have agree that the appearance of Christ took place while Paul was on his way to Damascus with the purpose of arresting the Christians of that city. "While he was still on the road and nearing Damascus, suddenly a light from the sky flashed all around him. He fell to the ground and heard a voice saying, 'Saul, Saul, why are you persecuting me?' 'Tell me, Lord,' he said, 'who you are.' The voice answered, 'I am Jesus, whom you are persecuting. But now get up and go into the city, and you will be told what you have to do" (Acts 9, 3 - 6). In another account, Christ is represented as making a fuller revelation to Paul: "... I have appeared to you for a purpose: to appoint you my servant and witness, to tell what you have seen and what you shall yet see of me. I will rescue you from your own people and from the Gentiles to whom I am sending you. You are to open their eyes and to turn them from darkness to light ... so that they may obtain forgiveness of sins and a place among those whom God has made his own through faith in me" (Acts 26, 16 - 18).

Hearing these words, both Paul and his companions were deeply perturbed and were completely at a loss for words in the face of what was happening. "Saul got up from the ground, but when he opened his eyes he could not see; they led him by the hand and brought him into Damascus. He was blind for three days and took no food or drink. There was in Damascus a disciple named Ananias. He had a vision in which he heard the Lord say: 'Ananias!' 'Here I am, Lord,' he answered. The Lord said to

him, 'Go to Straight Street, to the house of Judas, and ask for a man from Tarsus named Saul. You will find him at prayer; he has had a vision of a man named Ananias coming in and laying his hands on him to restore his sight.' Ananias answered, 'Lord, I have heard about this man and all the harm he has done to your people in Jerusalem. Now he is here with authority from the chief priests to arrest all who invoke your name.' But the Lord replied, 'You must go, for this man is my chosen instrument to bring my name before the nations and their kings and before the people of Israel. I myself will show him all that he must go through for my name's sake.' So Ananias went and, on entering the house, laid his hands on him and said, 'Saul, my brother, the Lord Jesus, who appeared to you on your way here, has sent me to you so that you may recover your sight and be filled with the Holy Spirit.' Immediately it was as if scales had fallen from his eyes, and he regained his sight. He got up and was baptized, and when he had eaten his strength returned" (Acts, 9, 8 - 18).

The divine intervention which occurred in the life and activities of Paul is truly beyond the comprehension of human reasoning, which finds it difficult to understand how a fanatical enemy of the Christians could so suddenly accept the word of Christ and, moreover, subsequently become the most tireless herald of it. Paul himself describes his conversion as a miracle from God: "I must make it clear to you, my friends, that the gospel you heard me preach is not of human origin. I did not take it over from anyone; no one taught it me; I received it through a revelation of Jesus Christ ... But then in his good pleasure, God, who from my birth had set me apart, and who had called me through his grace, chose to reveal his Son in and through me, in order that I might proclaim him among the Gentiles ..." (Gal. 1, 11 - 17). Nowhere in the epistles is there any suggestion of a gradual preparation of his soul for the vision which led him to Christianity.

Of course, Paul had been in contact with the preaching of the Apostles from the time of the stoning of the protomartyr Stephen. The profound conviction of the Christians that Jesus of Nazareth was the expected Messiah and their boldness in the face of persecution and torments would in all probability have had their psychological effect on him. Certain passages in the epistles could be taken to mean that Paul had met Christ before His Resurrection. "Am I not free? Am I not an apostle? Have I not seen Jesus our Lord?" (I Cor. 9, 1). However, certainty that this is the correct interpretation is lacking and this cannot be regarded as an established historical fact. What matters is that the vision on the Damascus road was a unique experience for Paul and turned his inner world upside down. For three days he was blind and took neither food or drink, unable to comprehend the transformation which was taking place. The appearance of Christ to him had brought about in a single moment the collapse of all the values on which he had built his life. In that moment he was completely thrown off course, his aims were overturned, and his spirit had to die in order to be raised again after three days. This 'resurrection' was at the same time a re-birth, accompanied by hope for the salvation of mankind.

After Paul had embraced Christianity and had begun his missionary journeys, he seems to have been very frequently troubled by the thought of what he had done before his conversion. The self-denial which marked his efforts to spread the Christian message was due in part to his making amends for his previous behaviour. "Last of all he appeared to me too: it was like a sudden, abnormal birth. For I am the least of the apostles, indeed not fit to be called an apostle, because I had persecuted the church of God. However, by God's grace I am what I am, and his grace to me has not proved vain; in my labours I have outdone them all - not I, indeed, but the grace of God working with me" (I Cor. 15, 8 - 11).

Immediately after his baptism, Paul went away into the region of Arabia Petrae, where in all likelihood he took the opportunity of gaining a more profound understanding of the word of God, of grasping with his intellect what he had accepted in his soul. According to another view, he began to preach immediately in the area around Damascus, which was also called 'Arabia'. When he returned to the city of Damascus, he threw himself with zeal into the work of spreading the Gospel, thus stirring up the hostility of the Jews, who saw their fanatical champion preaching the message which up to that point he had fought so strenuously against. Before long, seeing him as a threat to their religion, they resolved that he should be put to death. "When I was in Damascus, the commissioner of King Aretas kept the city under observation to have me arrested; and I was let down in a basket, through a window in the wall; and so I escaped his clutches" (II Cor. 11, 32 - 33). Aretas IV Philodemus held Damascus and other areas of Judaea between the years 37 and 40 AD. This fact leads to the conclusion that the conversion of Paul to Christianity took place in 35 - 36 AD, while his escape from Damascus must have been before 40 AD.

Paul next visited Jerusalem, where, as he tells us himself, he arrived three years after he was called by God (Gal. 1. 18 - 19). There, through the good offices of Barnabas he met the Apostles and formed a close relationship with them. Here his life was threatened for a second time and, after seeing a vision of Christ, he fled to Caesarea and Tarsus. Later, he visited Antioch and, after delivering, together with Barnabas, funds collected for its support to the church in Jerusalem, returned there. It was from Antioch that the spread of Christianity throughout the world was to begin. The Apostle Paul, having now believed in Christ with his heart and mind, set a new and single purpose in his life: the preaching of Christianity - "Of this gospel I have been appointed herald, apostle, and teacher" (II Tim. 1, 11).

Saint Paul, icon in the Byzantine and Christian Museum

THE PREACHING
OF PAUL

"From Paul, servant of Jesus Christ, called by God to be an apostle and set apart for the service of his gospel. This gospel God announced beforehand in sacred scriptures through his prophets. It is about his Son: on the human level he was a descendant of David, but on the level of the spirit -the Holy Spirit- he was proclaimed Son of God by an act of power that raised him from the dead: it is about Jesus Christ our Lord. Through him I received the privilege of an apostolic commission to bring people of all nations to faith and obedience in his name, including you who have heard the call and belong to Jesus Christ" (Rom. 1, 1 - 5).

The whole of the preaching of Paul, as we know it from the surviving sources, turns upon the Incarnation and Resurrection of Jesus Christ, who from being the object of Paul's persecution, became the absolute end of his life and work. Since Christ had revealed to him His sacrifice for the human race, he in his turn felt the obligation to reveal it to the whole world.

Paul never ceased to proclaim the sacrifice which God had required of His Son in order to drive out sin from mankind. No one in the world was of himself righteous and faithful to the word of God and the only salvation for sinners was in Christ's message of hope. "But Christ died for us while we were yet sinners, and that is God's proof of his love towards us. And so, since we have now been justified by Christ's sacrificial death, we shall all the more certainly be saved through him from final retribution ... we were reconciled to him through the death of his Son ... It was through one man that sin entered the world, and through sin death ... as the result of one misdeed was condemnation for all people, so the result of one righteous act is acquittal and life for all. For as through the disobedience of one man many were

made sinners, so through the obedience of one man many will be made righteous" (Rom. 5, 8 - 19). The incarnation and the death of Christ on the cross had been determined long before His birth, before the creation of the world. The Son of God, the Messiah of the prophets, was made man for the salvation of mankind and thus formed the bridge between the heavenly powers and those on earth.

22. Basilica B at Philippi, about 540 AD

The teaching of Paul extended beyond the incarnation, since the redemptive work of Christ was completed by His resurrection. The triumph over death demonstrated to all His divine origin and foreshadowed the resurrection of the dead. "For the trumpet will sound, and the dead will rise imperishable, and we shall be changed. This perishable body must be clothed with the imperishable, and what is mortal with immortality ... then the saying of scripture will come true: 'Death is swallowed up; victory is won!' 'O Death, where is your victory? O Death, where is your sting? ... But thanks be to God! He gives us victory through our Lord Jesus Christ" (I Cor. 15, 52 - 57).

According to Paul, the first step to establish communication with Christ is achieved through the sacrament of baptism. Those who are baptized become partakers in the Passion and Crucifixion, and have the hope that they will be raised from the dead as Jesus was. Paul himself was baptized by Ananias immediately after his conversion, but he himself baptized very few as Christians. " ... I did of course baptize the household of Stephanas; I cannot think of anyone else. Christ did not send me to baptise, but to proclaim the gospel" (I Cor. 1, 16 - 17). Nevertheless, in one of these instances, baptism was accompanied by the immediate manifestation of the Holy Spirit. As we are told by the Acts of Apostles, when Paul was at Ephesus he baptised some twelve persons as Christians and they at once began to speak in tongues and to prophecy.

In parallel with his skill as a public speaker, Paul possessed the ability to perform miracles, by which he was able to demonstrate to all the power which was given to him by his faith in God: "I will venture to speak only of what Christ has done through me to bring the Gentiles into his allegiance, by word and deed, by the power of signs and portents, and by the power of the Holy Spirit" (Rom. 15, 18 - 19).

Nor did he ever cease to maintain that the inner voice which guided him was the very voice of Christ. "For me life is Christ" (Phil. 1, 21). Although this conception was the driving force of his work, it never led him to show arrogance and self-regard: "After all, what is Apollos? What is Paul? Simply God's agents in bringing you to faith. Each of us performed the task which the Lord assigned to him: I planted the seed, and Apollos watered it, but God made it grow" (I Cor. 3, 5 - 6). It was only when it was necessary for him to urge on and encourage the Christians that he put forward his own labours as an example: "Follow my example, as I follow Christ's" (I Cor. 11, 1).

In his efforts to strengthen the faith of his hearers, Paul was transformed into a fiery orator, one who was guided more by the language of his soul than by orators' figures of speech. "The word I spoke, and the gospel I proclaimed, did not sway you with clever arguments; it carried conviction by spiritual power, so that your faith might be built not on human wisdom but on the power of God" (I Cor. 2, 4 - 5). Nonetheless, he often had recourse to parables in order to present in picture language the deeper concepts of Christianity. It was particularly when he spoke of love and of unity between human beings that his language became eloquent, virtually that of the poet, so that he could touch even the hardest of hearts. "I may speak in tongues of men or of angels, but if I have no love, I am a sounding gong or a clanging cymbal. I may have the gift of prophecy and the knowledge of every hidden truth; I may have faith enough to move mountains; but if I have no love I am nothing. I may give all I possess to the needy, I may give my body to be burnt, but if I have no love I gain nothing by it. Love is patient and kind. Love envies no one, is never boastful, never conceited, never rude; love is never selfish, never quick to take offence. Love keeps no score of wrongs, takes no pleasure in the sins of others, but delights in the truth. There is nothing which love cannot face; there is no limit to its faith, its hope, its endurance." (I Cor. 13, 1 - 7). And if he thought that sin had gained the upper hand over the word of God, he could become a severe and uncompromising speaker: " ... to those who sinned before, and to everyone else, I repeat the warning I gave last time; on my second visit I gave it in person, and now I give while absent. It is that when I come this time, I will show no leniency ... Our prayer to God is that you may do no wrong ... my aim is to spare myself, when I do come, any sharp exercise of authority -authority which the Lord gave me for building up and not for pulling down" (II Cor. 13, 2 - 10).

In spite of his enthusiasm and dedication, Paul was not an utopian romantic, out of touch with reality. His letters show that he had profound psychological insight and a unique skill in adaptation to his audience. "To Jews I behaved like a Jew, to win Jews: that is, to win those under the law I behaved as if under the law, though not myself subject to the law. To win those outside that law, I behaved as if outside the law, though not myself outside God's law, but subject to the law of Christ. To the weak I became weak, to win the weak. To them all I have become everything in turn, so that in one way or another I may save some" (I Cor. 9, 20 - 22). Paul also had the gift of being able to make a shrewd analysis of a situation and to exploit it accordingly in order to achieve his ends. Thus when the Romans arrested him in Jerusalem, he did not hesitate to make use of the privileges which derived fom his origins, in order to mollify his judges and his accusers. By stating that he was a Jew, he obtained permission to make his defence; his Roman citizenship rescued him from a flogging, and by proclaiming that as a Pharisee he believed in the resurrection of the dead, he ensured the support of the Pharisees in the crowd (Acts, Chaps. 21 - 23). When the high priest Ananias ordered his servants to strike Paul on the mouth, he answered him menacingly with the words: "God will strike you, you whitewashed wall! You sit there to judge me in accordance with the law; then, in defiance of the law, you order me to be struck!" (Acts 23, 3). This reaction was far from being the result of cowardice or fear in the face of danger. Paul's only concern was that he should succeed in

25. The Doric Temple of Apollo at ancient Corinth, about 540 BC

preaching yet again the word of God. He also knew that his work was not yet finished and that mankind had need of him alive and free.

Moreover, Paul had never given ground in the face of the hardships which he encountered and which, anyway, were the result of his own choices: "That is the reason for my present plight; but I am not ashamed of it, because I know whom I have trusted, and I am confident of his power to keep safe what he has put into my charge until the great day" (2 Tim. 1, 12). The pas-sion with which he justified the task which he had undertaken gave him not only boldness but immense satisfaction, so that any adversity could be cancelled out by the happiness he experienced in serving God. From the day of his conversion, Paul realised that in the work which he had undertaken he would encounter obstacles and difficulties, but he was prepared to renounce every wordly pleasure in order to gain heavenly life. "For me life is Christ, and death is gain. If I am to go on living in the body there is fruitful work for me to do. Which then I am to choose? I cannot tell. I am pulled two ways: my own desire is to depart and be with Christ -that is better by far; but for your sake the greater need is for me to remain in the body ... so that on my account you may have even more cause for pride in Christ Jesus - through seeing me restored to you" (Phil. 1, 21 - 26).

One of the hardest trials which Paul imposed upon himself was the earnest effort which he made to maintain himself without being a financial burden on anyone and without accepting any material reward for his preaching. He preferred to undergo any deprivation rather than give anyone grounds for accusing him of selfish or base motives. " ... We did not accept free hospitality from anyone; night and day in toil and drudgery we worked for a living, rather than be a burden to any of you -not because we do not have the right to maintenance, but to set an example for you to follow. Already during our stay with you we laid down this rule: anyone who will not work shall not eat" (2 Thess. 3, 8 - 10). In order to understand Paul's attitude over this matter we have to bear in mind that in his time a host of bogus teachers, philosophers and evangelists followed a wandering life, preaching redemption, with the sole purpose of their own -

chiefly material- gain. Paul was a vigorous opponent of all these 'false brethren' and constantly issued warnings to the Christians of the danger they were in of being led astray: "I implore you, my friends, keep an eye on those who stir up quarrels and lead others astray, contrary to the teaching you received. Avoid them; such people are servants not of Christ our Lord but of their own appetites, and they seduce the minds of simple people with smooth and specious words" (Rom. 16, 17 - 18). Naturally, they often reacted violently to Paul's admonitions and sought to undermine his work.

Apart from this, Paul's preaching frequently caused a more general hostility -not only on the part of Gentiles and Jews, but also of Christians themselves, many of whom accused him of distorting the essence of Christianity, a view which is not without its supporters- albeit few in number - among scholars even today. Others attempted to rob Paul of his authority by spreading rumours about the sums of money which he collected for the churches. For this reason, whenever he was carrying the proceeds of collections he took care to be accompanied by witnesses. However, his most fanatical opponents continued to be found among the Jews, who regarded him as an apostate and a threat to their religion. It was the Jews who were responsible for persecuting him, for attempts on his life, and for his final arrest in Jerusalem. "I implore you by our Lord Jesus Christ and by the love that the Spirit inspires, be my allies in the fight; pray to God for me that I may be saved from unbelievers in Judaea ..." (Rom. 15, 30 - 31).

Nevertheless, no obstacle proved capable of diminishing his enthusiasm or of deterring him from his chosen task. His efforts were strengthened by the support of those Christians who accorded him their respect and love. "There were loud cries of sorrow from them all, as they folded Paul in their arms and kissed him; what distressed them most was his saying that they would never see his face again. Then they escorted him to the ship" (Acts 20, 37 - 38).

27. Apostles, detail from a mosaic in the Monastery of Daphni, about 1100 AD

29. Detail from a mosaic in the Monastery of Daphni, about 1100 AD

THE APOSTLE OF THE GENTILES

The Apostle Paul made four journeys which took him to almost all the countries which ring the Mediterranean. In the course of these he succeeded in greatly increasing the number of Christian believers and founded the first Christian churches. The route which he followed among the Gentiles was systematically organised and soon took on the nature of a mission. He was not alone in this: apart from Paul, a large number of Christians whose names are unknown to us strove unceasingly to spread the Christain truth. Most of these unknown preachers, and the Apostles themselves, had formed a plan of joint action before Paul's conversion. Thus, when he was accepted into the Christian community, he followed the principles which the first Christians had already laid down.

Within this context, Paul attempted to select for his preaching those regions where the Name of Christ was not yet known. "But I have always made a point of taking the gospel to places where the name of Christ has not been heard, not wanting to build on another man's foundation: as scripture says, Those who had no news of him shall see, and those who never heard of him shall understand" (Rom. 15, 20 - 21). The first churches were founded in large and populous cities which soon became the centres from which the Christian message spread into the provinces. Close bonds developed between these churches, while Paul himself, by means of visits, his letters, and in person kept an eye on their progress and informed them of his own activities. Most of his epistles were written in order to encourage them in their efforts, to suggest solutions to their problems, and to convey to them the teachings of Christianity. Their contents give us a clear picture of the fervour and the love with which St Paul both admonished and supported the members of the churches. "I am not writing this to shame you, but to bring you to reason; for you are my dear children. You may have thousands of tutors in Christ, but you have only one father; for in Christ Jesus you are my offspring, and mine alone, through the preaching of the gospel. I

appeal to you therefore to follow my example. That is why I have sent Timothy, who is a dear son to me and a trustworthy Christian, to remind you of my way of life in Christ, something I teach everywhere in all the churches" (I Cor. 4, 14 - 17).

Paul's journeys and his tireless efforts rapidly bore fruit. The number of Christian communities increased and their membership constantly grew. The dissemination of Christianity among the Gentiles owed its success not only to the dedication of the Apostles, and particularly Paul, but also to the special political and social conditions of the time.

The missionary work of the early Christians was favoured above all by the administrative unity of the vast Roman Empire. The expansion of the Romans into the East and the West brought into contact two differing cultures and gave impetus to the spread of new ideas and attitudes. The long peace and conditions of normality which prevailed in the first and second centuries AD gave the Empire a cosmopolitan character and encouraged communication between its provinces. The Roman emperors, with the purpose chiefly of maintaining control over the territories which they had conquered, improved road and maritime communications, thus facilitating the spread of new theories to every region of the Mediterranean.

In the field of religion, the ground for the acceptance of new beliefs had been prepared as far back as the Hellenistic period, in which an amalgamation of elements of religion of varied origin had taken place. Following the same tradition, the Roman state showed marked toleration towards the manifestation and intermingling of varying religious trends. Within this context, the Western world came into contact with the mystery cults and the religions of the East, such as Mithraism and Judaism. At the same time, the ancient Greek divinities had begun to show symptoms of decline and worshippers preferred to direct their devotions to 'unknown gods' or to all the deities together (the Pantheon). The decline of the ancient cults led by degrees to the prevalence of monotheistic ideas, which were, moreover, reinforced by the Greek philosophy of the period. As early as the third century BC, when the Old Testament was translated into Greek, the monotheistic religion of the Jews was known to the Greeks. In Hellenistic times, Judaism was even more widely disseminated, thanks to the Jews of the Diaspora. Alexander the Great's successors, in organising the Greek states of the East, permitted the Jews to form independent communities, on condition that they used the Greek language. It was at this point that the Greeks started to be influenced by the Jewish religion, whilst their own culture had its effect on Judaism. The increasing familiarity with the idea of a single god which resulted was of decisive importance for the understanding of the Christian message on the part of the Gentiles.

Equally important for the spread of Christianity was the use of a single language by the inhabitants of the Roman state. This language was, of course, Greek, which had acquired this role by degrees since the time of Alexander's conquests. Apart from the regions which at an earlier date had belonged to the Hellenstic kingdoms, the West employed Greek in parallel with Latin, since the Romans were educated in Greek philosophy and thought. Thus Greek rapidly became a common ('koine') international language which could be studied in the numerous Greek schools which operated on Roman territory. It was for this reason that an excellent knowledge of Greek was a unique advantage for Paul, of paramount importance for the success of his work. Apart from this, the Greek language, the language of philosophy and rhetoric, made possible the most effective externalisation of the more profound concepts and ideas - such as those of Christianity.

Paul, in spite of his acquaintance with the language and spirit of the Greeks, was not favourably disposed towards their religion: " ... knowing God, they have refused to honour him as God, or to render him thanks. Hence all their thinking has ended in futility, and their misguided minds are plunged in darkness. They boast of their wisdom, but they have made fools of themselves, exchanging the glory of the immortal God for an image shaped like mortal man, even images like birds, beasts, and reptiles ... They have exchanged the truth of God for a lie, and have offered reverence and worship to created things instead of to the Creator. Blessed is he for ever. Amen" (Rom. 1, 21 - 25). The way in which the Greeks approached the world was, for Paul, defective, since it did not permit them to form the concept of the supreme essence of the cosmos, the concept of the One God, creator of all things. Their inability to grasp the meaning of the incarnation and resurrection of Christ proved the inferiority of their philosophy to the wisdom of God. The only way for Greek thought to be perfected was for it to be revised through the teaching of Christianity.

In no circumstances did the Apostle Paul exclude the Gentiles from his preaching. On the contrary, he visited first of all Greek cities, in the knowledge that the Greeks were always willing to learn about any new theory. It would seem that Paul, together with Barnabas, was the first to have the idea of approaching the Gentiles by means of missionary methods. For that reason they visited areas where the ancient Greek religion survived and preached Christianity to the Gentiles in exactly the same way as they did to the Jews. " ... There is no distinction between Jew and Greek, because the same Lord is Lord of all, and has riches enough for all who call on him" (Rom. 10, 12).

This approach brought Paul into conflict with the theology of the Pharisees, according to which man is justified with God only if he observes the Law to the letter. In transposing their justification from the Law to the person of Jesus Christ, Christians were able to receive into their communion those who did not observe, or did not even know, the Law. Another issue which arose in connection with Gentile converts to Christianity was that of circumcision, which was the subject of lengthy debate and which was finally resolved at the Council of Jerusalem of 49 AD. At this the Apostles determined that Gentiles who had embraced Christianity were under no obligation to be circumcised or to follow the Mosaic Law. Paul, who took part in the Council, applauded this decision and constantly proclaimed it to Gentiles and Jews alike. " ... Each one should accept the lot which the Lord has assigned him and continue as he was when God called him. That is the rule I gave in all the churches. Was a man called with the marks of circumcision on him? Let him not remove them. Was he uncircumcised when he was called? Let him not be circumcised. Circumcision or uncircumcision is neither here nor there: what matters is to keep God's commandments" (I Cor. 7, 17 - 19).

The freedom given by the Apostolic Council on the matter of the Law and of circumcision opened up the way for the conversion to Christianity of ever-increasing numbers of Gentiles. Paul treated all Christians as equal, regardless of their origins, though he thought that for the salvation of the Jews the example of the Gentiles who embraced the word of Christ would be necessary: "There is a divine secret here, my friends, which I want to share with you ... this partial hardening has come on Israel only until the Gentiles have been admitted in full strength; once that has happened, the whole of Israel will be saved ... Just as formerly you were disobedient to God, but now have received mercy because of their disobedience, so now, because of the mercy shown to you, they have proved disobedient, but only in order that they too may receive mercy" (Rom. 11, 25 - 31). In the Epistle to the Ephesians Paul gives a detailed account of the way in which God has granted his mercy to all mankind, without discriminating between Jew and Gentile: through the sacrifice of Christ He has offered concord and redemption to all. "Once you were far off, but now in union with Christ Jesus you have been brought near through the shedding of Christ's blood. For He is himself our peace. Gentiles and Jews, he has made the two one, and in His own body of flesh and blood has broken down the barrier of enmity which separated them ... This was His purpose, to reconcile the two in a single body to God through the cross, by which He killed the enmity" (Eph. 2, 13 - 16). Nevertheless, in Paul's eyes there was always one difference between the two peoples: the Jews took precedence in Christianity because

it was from them that the Messiah had been born and it was to them that He first entrusted His teaching. " ... There is a great grief and unceasing sorrow in my heart. I would even pray to be an outcast myself, cut off from Christ, if it would help my brothers, my kinsfolk by natural descent. They are descendants of Israel, chosen to be God's sons; theirs is the glory of the divine presence, theirs the covenants, the law, the temple worship, and the promises. The patriarchs are theirs, and from them by natural descent came the Messiah. May God, supreme above all, be blessed for ever! Amen" (Rom. 9, 2 - 5). The precedence of the Jews did not, of course, prevent the community of Christ from accepting new members regardless of origin or from expelling those who showed themselves faithless, whether Jews or Greeks. It was through such an approach that Paul succeeded in 'transplanting' Christianity from the Jewish to the Greek world and in making it a religion for all nations: " ... Those who were not my people I will call my people" (Rom. 9, 25).

30. The Parthenon on the Acropolis of Athens, 5th century BC. In front: the Odeon of Herod Atticus, 2nd century AD

THE FIRST JOURNEY: CYPRUS

ccording to the Acts of the Apostles, the missionary journeys of St Paul were decided upon by the same direct divine intervention as had brought about his conversion to Christianity: "There were in the church at Antioch certain prophets and teachers ... While they were offering worship to the Lord and fasting, the Holy Spirit said, 'Set Barnabas and Saul apart for me, to do the work to which I have called them.' Then, after further fasting and prayer, they laid their hands on them and sent them on their way" (Acts 13, 1 - 3). Their first journey took in Cyprus, Perga in Pamphylia, Antioch in Pisidia and the cities of Iconium, Lystra and Derbe. Paul's companion and the chief organiser of this expedition was Barnabas of Cyprus, a Greek Jew, who had been converted to Christianity at an early

stage. Barnabas had worked zealously to consolidate the newly-established church at Antioch and had been instrumental in bringing about the first meeting between Paul and the Apostles in Jerusalem. After the first journey was completed, he continued on his own and visited Cyprus for a second time. It was there that, at a much later date, he was put to death by stoning.

The two missionaries seem to have started on their journey in 47 BC and to have finished it two years later. Setting out from Seleucia in Syria, they landed on Cyprus at Salamis, one the island's largest ports. After teaching in the Jewish synagogues, they visited a large number of cities, coming eventually to Paphos. There Paul at-

tracted to Christianity the governor, Sergius Paulus, and performed his first recorded miracle by blinding the unbelieving sorcerer Elymas Bar-Jesus, who was attempting to put obstacles in the way of Paul's preaching. Although no Christian church was set up in Cyprus at this time, it would seem that there was some response to their teaching, at least in Paphos, where the Roman governor himself took an interest in it.

Cyprus, one of the Mediterranean's most beautiful islands, has had a long and troubled history. The first indications of human habitation date from the Neolithic period (6000 - 3000 BC), when the important 'Choirokoitia civilisation' developed. The first Greeks to penetrate into Cyprus (fourteenth to twelfth century BC) were Mycenaeans. They established themselves peacefully, but their influence was so strong that the whole island was rapidly Hellenised and retained its Mycenaean tradition for many centuries. The Greek myths provide ample information about the colonisation of the two cities which the Apostle Paul was later to visit. Thus, according to the Homeric epics, Salamis on Cyprus was founded by Teucer, who was son of Telamon, king of the Greek island of Salamis. The colonisation of Salamis - and of Paphos - took place immediately after the end of the Trojan War. After Troy fell, a storm brought to Cyprus Agapenor, admiral of the fleet from the Arcadia region of Greece. He drove out the city's

king, Cinyras, and became master of it himself. It was, of course, at Paphos that, according to tradition, the goddess Aphrodite was born.

The strategic position of Cyprus and its rich deposits of copper made the island the object of the territorial ambitions of its neighbours. Thus in historical times it was conquered successively by the Assyrians, the Egyptians, the Phoenicians and the Persians. In the fifth century BC it was liberated by the Athenians and Spartans, and until the late fourth century experienced a period of prosperity under King Euagoras of Salamis and his successors. The Persians, however, never ceased to covet Cyprus and all the power of Alexander the Great was needed to neutralise their threat. In return,

the Cypriots made their island over to him, and on his death, in 323 BC, it passed into the hands of the Ptolemies of Egypt. After 58 BC it was taken successively by the Romans, the Saracens, the Byzantines, the Franks, the Venetians, the Turks and the British. In 1960 Cyprus gained its independence, but today some 40% of its territory is occupied by the Turks as a result of their invasion of July 1974.

Apart from its unique natural beauty, the modern visitor can admire what has remained of the works of the peoples who

35. Cyprus, Kourion, view from the Sanctuary of Apollo

36. Cyprus, Paphos, medieval buildings

37. Cyprus, Kourion, the Temple of Apollo

have passed through Cyprus. Each of its cities still retains the impressions made by its individual history. Of these, Paphos combines a picturesque landscape with a large number of historical monuments. Remains of the ancient city and of the Temple of Aphrodite, much famed in antiquity, have come to light at what is today the village of Kouklia, while nine kilometres further on, at 'Petra tou Romiou', the local people point out the stretch of the shore where Aphrodite was born from the sea foam. Fifteen kilometres to the northwest of ancient Paphos is New Paphos, which was an extension of the ancient city and served in Roman times as the headquarters of the governors of the island. Archaeologists have discovered here a large number of prehistoric buildings and a luxurious residence of the third century BC, adorned with mosaic floors, the so-called 'House of Dionysus'. It was in this city, flooded with the memories of Greek antiquity, that Paul and Barnabas succeeded in delivering a new message of salvation, that of Christianity.

Of the other city which they are recorded as visiting, Salamis, some relics remain. These, however, are in the occupied territory of Cyprus.

FROM PAPHOS TO ANTIOCH - JERUSALEM

On leaving Paphos, Paul and Barnabas crossed over to Perga in Pamphylia, and from there continued their journey to Pisidian Antioch. There Paul preached the Gospel twice, both to the Jews and to the Gentiles, and seems to have succeeded in convincing many of his hearers, but the effectiveness of his words was equalled by the fury of the Jews, who drove them out

39. (below) Cyprus,
medieval fortress at the port of Paphos

38-39. Cyprus, the
Church of
Chrysopolitissa (St
Kyriaki), 15th
century AD

of the region. They also behaved in a similar manner in the next city, Iconium, where the population were divided into two factions, one supporting Paul and Barnabas and the other opposing them. Driven out of this city also, they made their way to Lystra. There, the Gentiles, hearing their teaching and seeing their miracles, thought that they were their gods visiting them in human form. Thus, they called Barnabas Zeus and Paul Hermes and made ready to offer sacrifices to them. Yet again, the reaction of the Jews was the exact opposite: they went so far as to stone Paul and to leave him unconscious, and, thinking that he was dead, were preparing to bury him. He, however, stood up unharmed, and left with his companion for Derbe. When Paul and Barnabas had completed their journey, they retraced their

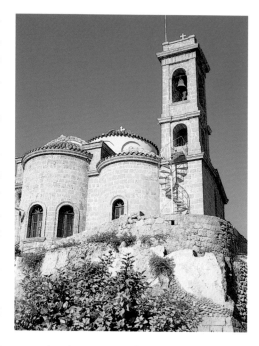

steps back to Antioch. The trials which Paul had undergone in Asia Minor seems to have had a decisive effect on his work and to have strengthened him even further in his faith. Naturally, his satisfaction in the fact that for the first time he saw his teaching being accepted by the Gentiles must have been great.

It was precisely this readiness of the Gentiles to accept Christianity which led Paul to raise the question of circumcision and obedience to the Jewish Law. It was to resolve this issue that a council of the Apostles was convened in Jerusalem in 49 BC. Paul and Barnabas took part in this

40. (below) Cyprus, Kourion, the Theatre, as it was reconstructed during the Roman period

41. Cyprus, a small church in the Troodos mountains

council and themselves conveyed its decisions in a letter to Antioch. According to these, neither observance of the Law nor circumcision was necessary for the salvation of a Christian. Throughout his life Paul remained faithful to the principles of this council and did not hesitate to rebuke the Apostle Peter himself when he thought that the latter showed signs of going back on them.

After the Council of Jerusalem, Paul and Barnabas preached the Gospel at Antioch and then decided to revisit the cities of Asia Minor. However, they were destined never to make this journey together, since as a result of a violent disagreement they chose to follow different routes.

42-43. (above) Cyprus, "Petra tou Romiou", the place where, according to tradition, Aphrodite was born

42-43. (below) Cyprus, Larnaca, a lagoon by the road from Salamis to Paphos

SECOND JOURNEY
THE VISION AT TROAS

While he was at Antioch, Paul made the acquaintance of Silas from Jerusalem, who subsequently accompanied him on his second journey. This began in Syria and Cilicia and took them to the cities of Lycaonia, Derbe and Lystra. At Lystra, " ... he found a disciple named Timothy, the son of a Jewish Christian mother and a gentile father, well spoken of by the Christians at Lystra and Iconium. Paul wanted to take him with him when he left ..." (Acts 16, 1 - 3). Timothy was to become a close associate and travelling companion of Paul. They were imprisoned together in Rome and later Timothy accompanied him on his fourth journey. In the course of this, he was established at Ephesus as its bishop. Two of Paul's letters are addressed to Timothy with the purpose of encouraging him in his work.

Leaving Lystra, Paul, Silas and Timothy successfully preached Christianity in various cities of Phrygia, Galatia and Mysia and then set out towards the Troad. Ilium, once the kingdom of Priam, long associated with the events of the Trojan War, was to link its fate, and the fate of the whole of Greece, with Christianity. According to the Acts of the Apostles, it was the work of the Holy Spirit that the three travellers went to the Troad and abandoned their plan to go to Bythinia and other parts of Asia Minor. Thus, in 49 BC they arrived in the Troad, which had been in the possession of the Romans since 189 BC.

It was on this spot, the meeting-place between Greece and the East, that Paul's visits to the cities of Greece were ordained by God. "During the night a vision came to Paul: a Macedonian stood there appealing to him, 'Cross over to Macedonia and help us' " (Acts 16, 9). This vision, just like that on the Damascus road, proved of decisive importance for the spread of Christianity. Without loss of time, Paul made ready to go to Greece, knowing that the time had come for the message of Christ to

be preached in the home of the ancient Greek religion.

Immediately after the account of this vision, the narrative in the Acts of the Apostle changes from the third person to the second person plural ('we'), which indicates that from that point on the writer himself had been present at the events which he describes. It would seem that the Evangelist Luke met the other three in the Troad and accompanied them on the rest of their journey. Some scholars have suggested that the vision in the Troad is an indirect reference to the presence of Luke, whom Paul in all probability got to know in Antioch, Luke's birthplace. Luke was familiar with Greek culture and spoke Greek, while it seems that he was a doctor by profession: "Greetings to you from our dear friend Luke, the doctor" (Col. 4, 14). He accompanied Paul on his second and third journey and remained with him during his first imprisonment in Rome, as well as during the second, when everyone else had left him. " ... Demas ... has deserted me and gone to Thessalonica; Crescens is away in Galatia, Titus in Dalmatia; apart from Luke I have no one with me" (II Tim. 4, 10 - 11). According to tradition, Luke preached the Gospel in Gaul, Dalmatia, Italy and Greece and died, at the age of over 80, somewhere near Thebes.

45. The Trojan Horse, from a relief amphora in the Museum of Myconos, 8th - 7th century BC

46-47. The church in the Monastery of Hosios (Blessed) Lukas, 1011 AD

ARRIVAL IN GREECE
SAMOTHRACE - KAVALA

"We sailed from Troas and made a straight run to Samothrace, the next day to Neapolis ..." (Acts 16, 11).

These words are the only information we have about the first cities in Greece to accept the preaching of St Paul. We know nothing else about the voyage from Asia Minor or about his teaching there and its effect on the inhabitants. One thing is certain: this was the first time that the Name of Christ had been heard in the West and on European soil.

Samothrace is an exceptionally mountainous island near the coast of Thrace. Its highest peak, Fengari on Mt Saos (1800 m.), is covered with snow all the year round, while, if one excepts nearby Mount Athos, it stands at a greater height than all the surrounding regions. The nature of its terrain is such that level shorelines and harbours are very rare. In antiquity the only port was Demetrion, which has been identified with the present-day Kamariotissa bay. It is there that the vessel bringing Paul and his companions from the Troad must have anchored.

The oldest organised settlement to have been found on Samothrace, at Mikro Vouni on the south-western coast, was established in the Neolithic period, at the end of the fifth millennium BC and must have had some connection with the Pelasgians, who, according to Herodotus, were the island's first inhabitants. A second settlement was established in the Bronze Age on the acropolis of Vrichos, west of Chora, by Thracian tribes. The first Greeks to colonise Samothrace were Aeolians from Asia Minor or from Lesbos. Accord-

ing to tradition, Saon, son of Zeus or of Hermes, was its first ruler and lawgiver. He was responsible for the building of the city of Samothrace, which during the seventh and sixth centuries BC developed into an important commercial centre, minted its own silver coins and acquired a small fighting fleet. The island was taken in 513 BC by the Persians, while between 477 BC and the reign of Philip II it was dependent on the policy of Athens and Sparta. In Hellenistic times it passed into the hands of the Macedonian rulers Lysimachus, King of Thrace, the Ptolemies of Egypt, and the Seleucids of Syria. In 168 BC it was taken by the Romans.

Samothrace in historical times, and particularly in the Hellenistic period, was a Panhellenic religious centre of international prestige, thanks to the mystery cult there of the Great Gods. The gods of Samothrace, known as the Kabeiroi, were of pre-Greek origin. The Greeks identified them with their own Demeter, Persephone, Hades and Hermes, who presided over death and life after death. The central divinity, Axieros, had the characteristics of Demeter, the central figure in the Eleusinian Mysteries, which were performed in southern Greece. The festivals at the sanctuary of the Great Gods included mystery rites which prepared the faithful for life after death and ensured for them the protection of the Kabeiroi against the dangers of the sea. Philip II and his wife, Olympias, mother of

Alexander the Great, were initiated into the mysteries of the Kabbeiroi at an early age. The remains of the sanctuary of the Great Gods have been discovered in the north of the island, near the site of the ancient walled city of Samothrace. Among the buildings which have come to light are the Palace, which was used for the final phase of the mysteries, and the Arsenoeion, the largest known ancient Greek circular building, dedicated by Arsinoë, wife of Lysimachus, a little before 270 BC. Today, an archaeological museum stands on the site. This contains finds from the sanctuary and other sites. Notable among the exhibits is a copy of the famous Victory of Samothrace, the original of which is in the Lou-

vre. This statue of the winged personification of victory was found in 1863 during excavations carried out on the island by the French Consul, Champois, who himself took it to France.

In Byzantine times, Samothrace belonged to the Theme of Thrace until 1204, when it was captured by the Crusaders. Between the ninth and the fourteenth centuries AD the inhabitants gradually withdrew into the interior of the islands and built Chora, the chief

48. Samothrace, the Sanctuary of the Great Gods, 4th century BC

49. Byzantine bas-relief

50. Samothrace, the Tholos of Arsinoë (Arsinoeon), 3rd century BC

town of the island today, at a distance from the sea. In 1462 the island was taken by the Turks, who during the War of Independence of 1821 slaughtered all the male population and sold the women and children into slavery. Union with Greece, for which the islanders had striven for centuries, finally came in 1912. Today, Samothrace, well-watered and rich in wild woodland, is an ideal refuge for those who seek closer contact with nature.

Neapolis, the city which Paul visited immediately after Samothrace, is now known as Kavala. Ancient Neapolis was colonised by the Athenians in the fifth century BC and remained their ally until it was taken by Philip II in the mid fourth century BC. From then on it served as the port of the nearby city of Philippi and trade brought it prosperity down to the time of the dissolution of the Macedonian state. The visit of the Apostle Paul resulted in the arrival there of a large number of settlers from Jerusalem and a revival of its commercial activities. In the Byzantine period the inhabitants named their city 'Christoupolis', most probably to commemorate the early establishment of a Christian church there by the Apostle Paul. In the view of some scholars, it was in this period that a Byzantine church was built in the city, dedicated to St Paul. This was subsequently converted into a mosque by the Turks, who captured Kavala in 1380 and confined its population within the Byzantine fortress. It was only in the nineteenth century that the city was allowed to expand beyond the

confines of the fortress, a development which was associated with renewed prosperity for the city. In the Balkan Wars, Kavala fell into the hands of the Bulgarians, to achieve its final liberation in 1913.

Today, Kavala is a modern city with an important port, but the marks of its age-old character are still plain to see. The large squares and high modern buildings co-exist with the old, low houses in the traditional style, the gardens and the paved alleyways. The harbour is dominated by the Byzantine fortress, which crowns the amphitheatrical site of the city. This harbour is the main outlet for the export of tobacco from northern Greece; Greece's earliest tobacco factories were in Kavala. Among the sights worth seeing are the old aqueduct ('Kamares'), the work of

Suleyman the Magnificent (sixteenth century), the house of the Egyptian governor Mohamet Ali (1805 - 1848), who was born in Kavala, the Archaeological Museum, the large number of Byzantine churches, and the church which was built in 1928 to commemorate St Paul's visit.

51. Samothrace, the Sanctuary of the Great Gods, 4th century BC

52. Kavala, the aqueduct, work of Souleyman the Magnificent (16th century AD), which separates the old from the modern town

53. Kavala, view of the town with the old aqueduct and a traditional boatyard at the port

PHILIPPI

"... And from there to Philippi, a leading city in that district of
Macedonia and a Roman colony" (Acts 16, 12).

Paul would certainly have gone from Neapolis to Philippi by the Via Egnatia, which stretched from Apollonia on the Adriatic coast to the banks of
the River Hebrus, on the Aegean, passing through the cities which were of
importance at that time. In fact, the Via Egnatia was an extension of the
road which linked Rome with the city of Egnatia in Apulia; in Byzantine times it was
extended even further, as far as Constantinople. The central section of the road was
constructed in the second century BC and passed through the city of Philippi on its
way to Neapolis in the south-east and Amphipolis in the south-west.

Philippi lies some 17 kilometres to the south-west of Kavala, between Mt Pangaio and Mt Orvilos. It was first founded by colonists from the island of Thasos in
360/359 BC and was given the name of Krenides. The Thasians, who were extremely active in founding colonies along the shores of Thrace, chose to found
Krenides inland because of the importance of the site: the new city stood near the
silver and gold mines of Pangaio and Orvilos, in an area rich in agricultural and
forestry products and at a key point for the control of the roads in the interior of
Thrace. Four years after the foundation of the city, the Thasians were forced to seek
the intervention of Philip II to deal with the Thracian tribesmen of the region.
Philip, exploiting the opportunity, made himself lord of the city and named it after
himself. The city was taken by the Romans in 168 BC, while it was here in 42 BC
that Cassius and Brutus fought against Octavian and Antony. The victory of the latter two resulted in the settling here of new colonists -farmers and praetorian guards-
and the creation of a colony of importance, which was named Colonia Augusta Julia Philippiensis. Thus, what St Paul would have seen when he visited Philippi in 49
AD was a well developed city, predominantly Roman in character.

The remains of Philippi even today give some idea of the grandeur of the Roman city. All its buildings were enclosed by a strong wall, constructed in the time of Philip and repaired in the Byzantine period. The Via Egnatia passed through the fortified city by means of two of its three gates. In following the Via Egnatia, the paving of which is still visible, Paul would probably have entered the city by its eastern gate, the so-called Neapolis Gate. The city's principal buildings stood on either side of the Via Egnatia: to the north was the theatre, dating from the time of Philip II, a sanctuary to the Egyptian divinities, of the second century AD, and smaller open-air sanctuaries. On the southern side, the remains of a Roman market, its buildings dating from the second century, have been discovered. Among them are workshops, warehouses, administrative buildings, the tribune for public speakers, fountains and colonnades, a library and two small temples, dedicated to the Emperor Antoninus Pius and his wife, Faustina. Further south there was another market, a wrestling school of the second century, and Roman baths. Naturally, as most of the buildings which have been excavated belong to the second century AD, they cannot give a clear picture of what Philippi looked like in the time of Paul.

Paul stayed in Philippi for a number of days. His first concern was to make contact with Jews living there. However, there

cannot have been many Jews resident in Philippi, since nowhere do we find any mention of a synagogue. Moreover, in order to meet them, Paul had to leave the city and make his way to the river bank, where they gathered to pray. It was here that Lydia, a seller of textiles from Thyatira in Asia Minor, became the first woman to be baptized on European soil. " ... And on the Sabbath we went outside the city gate by the riverside, where we thought there would be a place of prayer; we sat down and talked to the women who had gathered there. One of those listening was called Lydia, a dealer in purple fabric, who came from the city of Thyatira; she was a worshipper of God, and the Lord opened her heart to respond to what Paul said. She was baptized, and her household with her, and then she urged us, 'Now that you have accepted me as a believer in the Lord, come and stay at my house.' And she insisted on our going" (Acts 16, 13 - 15). Near the archaeological site of Philippi there is a small river, a 'little Jordan', as it has been called, where it is believed that the baptism of Lydia took place. A small Christian church was erected on the spot in memory of the event and the place received the name of 'Lydia'.

55. Philippi, Basilica B, about 540 AD

56. Philippi, view of the Via Egnatia

57. Philippi, view of the Roman Agora

The hospitality of Lydia to Paul and his companions is typical of the love and mutual support which bound together the first Christians. Such ties of friendship were to be expected in a small community which had to face the hostility and persecution both of the Jews and of the state itself. Paul always urged the churches to draw courage and strength for their efforts from the concord and fraternal spirit of the Christians. "About love of the brotherhood you need no words of mine, for you are yourselves taught by God to love one another, and you are in fact practising this rule of love towards all your fellow-Christians throughout Macedonia. Yet we appeal to you, friends, to do better still. Let your ambition be to live quietly ..." (I Thess. 4, 9 - 11). For Paul, hospitality was an act of love: "Never cease to love your fellow-Christians. Do not neglect to show hospitality; by doing this, some have entertained angels unawares" (Heb. 13, 1 - 2). To the east of the archaeological site of Philippi two complexes of private houses, dating from the Roman period to the tenth century AD, were recently discovered. The house of Lydia, where Paul was entertained, may have been in this quarter, though tradition places it near the river where she was baptized.

Paul's stay at Philippi was not consistently peaceful: the inhabitants of the city persecuted, tortured and imprisoned him. "Once, on our way to the place of prayer, we met a slave-girl who was possessed by a spirit of divination and brought large profits to her owners by telling fortunes.

She followed Paul and the rest of us, shouting, 'These men are servants of the Most High God, and are declaring to you a way of salvation.' She did this day after day, until, in exasperation, Paul rounded on the spirit. 'I command you in the name of Jesus Christ to come out of her', he said, and it came out instantly. When the girl's owners saw that their hope of profit had gone, they seized Paul and Silas and dragged them to the city authorities in the main square; bringing them before the magistrates, they alleged, 'These men are causing a disturbance in our city; they are Jews, and they are advocating practices which it is illegal for us Romans to adopt and follow.' The mob joined in the attack; and the magistrate had the prisoners stripped and gave orders for them to be flogged. After a severe beating they were flung into prison and the jailer was ordered to keep them under close guard. In view of these orders, he put them into the inner prison and secured their feet in the stocks" (Acts 16, 16 - 24).

The account of the slave-girl with prophetic powers could be seen as suggesting the victory of Christianity over the religion of the heathen. The young soothsayer owed her powers to the spirit of the serpent Python which had possessed her. Python was associated with the ancient Greek oracle of Delphi, which was

59. (above) Philippi, the Roman Agora, where Saint Paul and Silas were flogged

59. (below) Philippi, view of the archeological site

renowned throughout the ancient world for the prophecies delivered by means of the Pythia priestess by the god Apollo. Before passing into the hands of Apollo, the Delphi oracle had been in the possession of another deity, Ghea, or Mother Earth, and had been guarded by the demon Python. Both Ghea and Python were personifications of the powers which the earth had to offer. But the power of Christ was able to conquer all, since to Him even the evil spirit of Python submitted. Immediately after this exorcism, the slave-girl ceased to prophecy and her masters resolved to take their revenge. The accusation made against Paul was carefully thought out and based on two arguments: the accused were of Jewish origin and were attempting to disrupt the peace of the city by teaching new religions. The Roman generals never allowed attempts to cause upheavals in the smooth running of the state to go unpunished, particularly if the perpetrators were not Roman citizens.

In the very same year they had expelled large numbers of Jews from Rome, the Empire's capital. The prison in which Paul and Silas were held stood, according to tradition, on the spot where the early Christian church known as Basilica A was later built. This account has not received confirmation, since the site under the

60-61 (above) Philippi, general view of the archeological site

60. (below) Philippi, Basilica A, about 500 AD

61. (left) Philippi, Byzantine capital

61. (right) Philippi, view of the Basilica B, about 540 AD

basilica has been shown to have been occupied by a Roman cistern.

Paul's imprisonment at Philippi did not last more than a few hours according to the account given in the Acts of the Apostles: "About midnight Paul and Silas, at their prayers, were singing praises to God, and the other prisoners were listening, when suddenly there was such a violent earthquake that the foundations of the jail were shaken; the doors burst open and all the prisoners found their fetters unfastened. The jailer woke up to see the prison doors wide open and, assuming that the prisoners had escaped drew his sword intending to kill himself. But Paul shouted, 'Do yourself no harm; we are all here.' The jailer called for lights, rushed in, and threw himself down before Paul and Silas, trembling with fear. He then escorted them out and said, 'Sirs, what must I do to be saved?' They answered, 'Put your trust in the Lord Jesus, and you will be saved, you and your household,' and they imparted the word of the Lord to him and to everyone in his house. At that late hour of the night the jailer took them and washed their wounds, and there and then he and his whole family were baptized. He brought them up into his house, set out a meal, and rejoiced with his whole household in his new-found faith in God. When daylight came, the magistrates sent their officers with the order, 'release those men.' The jailer reported these instructions to Paul: 'The magistrates have sent an order for your release. Now you are free to go in peace.' But Paul

said to the officers: ' We are Roman citizens! They gave us a public flogging and threw us into prison without trial. Are they now going to smuggle us out by stealth? No indeed! Let them come in person and escort us out.' The officers reported his words to the magistrates. Alarmed to hear that they were Roman citizens, they came and apologised to them, and then escorted them out and requested them to go away from the city. On leaving the prison they went to Lydia's house, where they met their fellow-Christians and spoke words of encouragement to them, and then they took their departure" (Acts 16, 25 - 40).

The miracle of the earthquake and the events of Paul and Silas's imprisonment would without doubt have been an over-whelming experience for the jailer, leading to his immediate conversion to Christianity. His household, together with Lydia, made up the first members of the Christian community at Philippi, the first Christian church to be established in Europe. Paul always retained feelings of deep affection for the church at Philippi, as can be seen for the letter which he sent there from Rome, during his imprisonment there, or from Ephesus. "From Paul and Timothy, servants of Christ Jesus, to all God's people at Philippi, who are incor-

62. Philippi, the place where, according to tradition, the prison of Saint Paul was located

63. Philippi, the Theatre. It was built by Philip II during the 4th century BC and reconstructed by the Romans in the second half of the 2nd century AD

porate in Christ Jesus, with the bishops and deacons. Grace to you and peace from God our Father and the Lord Jesus Christ. I thank my God every time I think of you; whenever I pray for you all, my prayers are always joyful, because of the part you have taken in the work of the gospel from the first day until now" (Phil. 11, 1 - 5). The church at Philippi stood by Paul in all his difficulties and frequently gave him its moral and material support: "You Philippians are aware that, when I set out from Macedonia in the early days of my mission, yours was the only church to share with me in the giving and receiving; more than once you contributed to my needs, even at Thessalonica" (Phil. 4, 15 - 16). The fact that in this case Paul went against his own principles in this matter and accepted their aid is proof of his regard for and absolute trust in the Christians of Philippi.

During the course of his third journey (52 - 56 AD), he revisited the cities of Macedonia. Although there is no clear reference to Philippi, it is reasonable to assume that he went there, given that the church there was so dear to him. On this occasion, he retraced his steps through Macedonia, so that it would seem that he visited Philippi three times in all. Even when he was elsewhere, he took care to keep himself informed of the affairs of the Philippians. Thus, during his imprisonment in Rome in 62 - 64 AD, the church at Philipppi sent him financial assistance by means of Epaphroditus, who fell gravely ill while in Rome. On his recovery, he returned to Philippi together with Timothy as bearer of the letter which Paul had written. There is, however, another version of events according to which the visit of Epaphroditus to Paul was not during the latter's imprisonment in Rome but to Ephesus in 54/55 AD.

After the triumph of Christianity, Philippi developed into a major city of strategic importance. In the Byzantine period a large number of Christian monuments were erected. To the present day, the ruins of no fewer than four early Christian basilicas can be seen on the archaeological site of Philippi, of which the most important is the so-called Basilica B, of the sixth century AD. The most striking of the city's early Christian monuments was the famous Octagon, an octagonal church, built in the late fourth century and rebuilt in the fifth and sixth. Excavations have revealed the greater part of the building, which some believe to have served as the cathedral of Philippi.

65. (above) Philippi, the place where, according to tradition, the baptism of Lydia took place. In the background a modern church, built in memory of the event

65 (below) A baptistery by the small river Gaggitis, on the spot where, according to tradition, Lydia was baptized

66. Amphipolis, the famous Lion of Amphipolis: according to the most probable explanation it crowned a funerary edifice, which was used as a burial place of one of Alexander's generals after the Asia campaign, 4th century BC

AMPHIPOLIS - APOLLONIA

"They travelled by way of Amphipolis and Apollonia and came to Thessalonica" (Acts 17, 1).

The fact that this sentence in the Acts of the Apostles is again written in the third person plural indicates that Luke did not accompany the others to Thessalonica. In fact, as emerges from the narrative, only Silas was with Paul, Timothy having remained at Philippi. Apart from this, nothing else is know about the visit to Amphipolis and Apollonia. However, it can be regarded as certain that they once again travelled from Philippi to Amphipolis, a distance of approximately 55 kilometres, along the Via Egnatia.

Amphipolis lies between Mounts Kerdylio and Pangaio, very close to the Strymon river. The region had been inhabited since Neolithic times and was known as 'Ennea Hodoi' (= Nine Roads). Down to the fifth century BC it belonged to the Thracian tribe of the Hedoni, who had frequently had to resist the expansionist aims of the Athenians. In 437 BC Ennea Hodoi fell into their hands and became an important Athenian colony, to which the name of Amphipolis was given. The subsequent development of Amphipolis was the result of its geographical position, at a key point on land and river communications, near Pangaio with its gold, and in the middle of the fertile plain of the Strymon. Before colonising Amphipolis itself, the Athenians had taken its port, Eion, five kilometres to the south, at the mouth of the Strymon, on the Strymonic Gulf. Eion was to remain in the hands of the Athenians when Amphipolis was captured by the Spartans under their general, Brasidas, during the Peloponnesian War. Brasidas and the Athenian general Cleon were killed there in 422 BC after a dramatic battle. From 421 BC until the time of Philip II (357 BC), the city remained independent, under the suzerainty of the Macedonians. In 334 BC, Alexander the Great set out on his expedition into Asia from here, having anchored his fleet along the length of the Strymon as far as the harbour of Eion. The Romans took Amphipolis in 168 BC and Aemilius Paulus made it the capital of one of the four provisional republics set up in Macedonia. In the first century BC it was destroyed by Thracian

tribesmen, to be rebuilt by Octavian, after which it retained its importance into the Byzantine period. Its decline began in the the sixth century BC, after which it dwindled into insignificance.

The classical city of Amphipolis was ringed by a double wall, of a length of 7.5 kilometres. Parts of the classical fortifications, and of the Hellenistic repairs to these, are visible today at some 80 points. At intervals, a large number of channels, to carry rainwater out of the city, built into the wall, have survived. From a technical point of view, this project was advanced for its time, its purpose being to cope with the flooding which could have destroyed the fortifications. In the course of archaeological investigations, five gates have been discovered in the walls. Three of these, on the north, are of the Classical period and the rest are Roman. One of the latter, the so-called South Gate, led to the Via Egnatia, and would have been

used by St Paul to enter the city. In the north-western part of the city, very close to the wall, a unique discovery was recently made -one which has a direct connection with events in the Peloponnesian War as described by the historian Thucydides. This is the famous bridge over the Strymon, whose substructure, with its wooden stakes, unique in Greece, has been preserved intact through the centuries. It was this very bridge that the Spartan general Brasidas crossed in 424 BC and which thus was a great help to him in his conquest of Amphipolis.

Excavations have brought to light a large number of private houses, dating from the fourth century BC to Hellenistic times, but very few public buildings. Among the latter are a gymnasium complex, in use from the fourth century BC, a theatre, a small temple to Demeter from the old city of Ennea Hodoi, a sanctuary to the Phrygian deities, and a sanctuary

dedicated to the Muse Clio. Of the funerary monuments the most striking are three Macedonian tombs of the third century BC and the famous Lion of Amphipolis. The most probable explanation of the latter, which has now been set up again, is that it crowned a funerary edifice which was used as the burial place of one of Alexander's generals after the Asia campaign in the fourth century BC.

Many of the buildings described above could have been seen when St Paul visited Amphipolis. However, the remains of the Roman city are too scanty to allow a reconstruction of what it looked like. By way of contrast, a wealth of monuments of the early Christian period, reflecting the success of Paul's preaching, have been excavated. The initial nucleus of the Christian community appears to have been formed at an early date, since Amphipolis became the see of a bishop as early as the third century and produced St Mocius, who was martyred under Diocletian. Today the remains of four early Christian basilicas and of a hexagonal sanctuary of the sixth century have survived.

The next stop of Paul and Silas was Apollonia, also reached by the Via Egnatia. This was some 45 kilometres west of Amphipolis, near the present-day village of Nea Apollonia. Apollonia was founded in the fifth century BC by Philip I and took its name from the god Apollo, patron of music, harmony and the mean. It's development was due to its strategic position between Amphipolis and Thessalonica and its proximity to Lake Volvi. The city was destroyed in barbarian invasions in the fifth and sixth centuries AD.

68. Amphipolis, view of the ancient fortification of the town 69. Amphipolis, the wooden stakes of the bridge over Strymon river, as they have been preserved from the Classical period

THESSALONIKI

Having passed through Amphipolis and Apollonia, Paul, still following the Via Egnatia, then travelled the 60 kilometres to Thessalonica (modern Thessaloniki). His short stay in these two places is understandable, since he knew that he was close to Thessaloniki, a city of exceptional importance, the capital of the Roman province of Macedonia.

The Thessaloniki region, at the head of the Thermaic Gulf, has a history which goes back thousands of years. The first known settlement here was in the Neolithic period; since then the area has been inhabited continuously down to the present time. Long before Thessaloniki was founded, the city of Therme, from which the Thermaic Gulf takes its name, stood in the same area. Although its exact position has not yet been identified, its existence is confirmed by a number of ancient sources. From the time of the arrival of the first Hellenes, in the Bronze Age, the settlements in the area -including Therme- maintained close contacts with southern Greece, exchanging material and intangible goods. The need for contact with the rest of the cities of Greece led the king of Macedonia, Cassander, to unite 26 townships on the Thermaic Gulf and to found a new city in 316/315 BC, to which he gave the name of his wife, the sister of Alexander the Great, Thessaloniki. The city was fortified and very rapidly developed into an important commercial and maritime centre. Very little has remained of the first phase of its history, but we know from the literary sources that it had a luxurious palace, an agora (marketplace), a gymnasium, and a large number of sanctuaries.

In 168 BC Thessaloniki was taken by the Romans and in 146 became capital of the province of Macedonia. In 42 BC it was declared a free city, with a democratic administration and the right to elect its own rulers and to mint its own coins. In the reign of Augustus it was a prosperous commercial and cultural centre, of a predominantly Greek, rather than Roman, character. By the beginning of the Christian era it

was a cultural Mecca which attracted men of letters and the arts, together with large numbers of immigrants, traders and craftsmen. It was against this background that the city's Jewish community, to which Paul addressed himself, was established. In 250 AD, under the Emperor Decius, Thessaloniki became a Roman colony, while in 297 the Emperor Galerius Maximian chose it as his seat of government and built his royal palace in the city. The complex of the palace buildings was in the south-eastern quarter of Thessaloniki and, apart from the main palace building, included the Rotunda, the Octagon, the Hippodrome, and the Arch of Galerius. The Rotunda, the most southerly of the buildings, served either as a temple or as the mausoleum of Galerius. Circular in shape, it was roofed by a dome. In the mid fifth century AD it was converted into a Christian church, dedicated to St George. It still stands today, in good condition, and is one of the 'sights' of the city. South of the Rotunda, the Arch of Galerius, known locally as the 'Kamara', is to be seen. This was set up by Galerius after his victory over the Persians as a symbol of his triumph. A road led through the Arch to the palace, a building of great luxury, its various apartments laid out around a central colonnaded courtyard. To the east was the Hippodrome, and further to the south, the Octagon, the most important building in the group, most probably used as a throne room.

In the second century AD, the Roman Forum of Thessaloniki was laid out. This consisted of two communicating squares, colonnades for commercial administrative uses, and an Odeion. Excavations have brought to light a large number of Roman baths, and the remains of the Via Regia, an extension of the Via Egnatia. The movable finds from the archaeological investigations are to be seen in the Thessaloniki Archaeological Museum.

In the Byzantine period, Thessaloniki continued to be prosperous and was an important Christian, as well as political and economic centre of Macedonia. From an early date the emperors of Byzantium made themselves benefactors of the city, following the lead of Constantine, who rebuilt its harbour. At the end of the fourth or in the early fifth century new solidly constructed walls were built, parts of which remain, in good condition, today. The fifth century saw the building of the Churches of St Demetrius, Our Lady 'Acheiropoietos', and the Blessed David (Latomos Monastery). The basilica of St Demetrius was built on the site of Roman baths, on the exact spot where, according to tradition, the saint was martyred in 303 AD. It is a major treasure of Christian art, both in terms of its architecture

71-72. Thessaloniki, the White Tower, part of the medieval fortifications of the town

73. Thessaloniki, the Diikitiriou Square in the center of the town

and of its carved and mosaic decoration. Mosaic compositions of importance are preserved in all the churches mentioned above, as well as in that of St George (Rotunda). It was over the site of a basilica of the same period that the Church of Holy Wisdom (Aghia Sophia), in the style of a domed basilica, was built in the seventh century and decorated with equally fine mosaics and wall-paintings.

Between the sixth and the eleventh centuries, Thessaloniki was subjected to repeated raids by the Slavs, the Arabs, Saracen pirates, and the Bulgars. In 995, the Tsar of the Bulgars, Samuel, defeated the Byzantine army and took the city, which was recovered by Byzantium after the victories of Basil II 'the Bulgar-Slayer' between 1014 and 1019. This was followed by a period of tranquillity and development in every field. In was during this time that the Church of Our Lady Chalkeon ('of the Coppersmiths') (1028) was built. This is in the cross-in-square

style with a dome, and combines the trends in architecture of southern Greece with those of Constantinople. The twelfth century was marked by Norman raids, and after the capture of Constantinople by the Franks in 1204, Thessaloniki was surrendered to Boniface of Montferrat. In the 1223, the Despot of Epirus, Theodore Angelus, put an end to Latin rule over Constantinople and was himself crowned king. In 1261, after Constantinople had been recovered, Thessaloniki passed once

74-75. (above) Thessaloniki, the Rotunda, Roman building served either as a temple or as the mausoleum of the Emperor Galerius (306-311 AD). In the 5th century AD it was converted into a Christian church, dedicated to St George

74. (below) Thessaloniki, the Church of St Sophia (Holy Wisdom), 7th century AD

75. (below left) Thessaloniki, the Basilica of St Demetrius, second half of the 5th century AD

75. (below right) Thessaloniki, the Church of the Prophet Elias, 14th century AD

again into the hands of the Byzantines. During the period of the Palaeologues it experienced a period of prosperity, which was marked by considerable building activity. The Churches of the Holy Apostles, St Catherine, St Pantaleimon, and St Nicholas 'Orphanos', the chapel of St Euthymius in the Basilica of St Demetrius, and the Vlatades Monastery all belong to this period. The churches of Thessaloniki make up a veritable treasure-house of Christian art, covering all the phases of

76. Thessaloniki, part of the Vlatades Monastery, 1360-1370 AD

77. (above) Thessaloniki, the Church of St Nicholas "Orphanos", early 14th century AD

77. (below) Thessaloniki, the Church of Our Lady "Chalkeon", 1028 AD

the Byzantine age. The movable finds dating from this period are housed in the city's Byzantine Museum.

After seven years of Venetian rule, Thessaloniki was taken by the Turks in 1430. From the late fifteenth century it was the home of a large Jewish community, which in the century which followed made a major contribution to the city's material and cultural advance. In 1821, Thessaloniki played an active part in the Greek War of Independence, while in 1903 - 1904 it became the centre for the Macedonian Struggle. The city's final liberation from the Turks came in 1912, to be followed by a major fire in 1917, with subsequent extensive rebuilding.

Today, Thessaloniki, the 'Bride of the Thermaic', has the second largest population in Greece. It is an important commercial, industrial, communications and tourist centre, while it has a large number of academic institutions and university faculties. Its cultural life is particularly vigorous, thus continuing a tradition which goes back thousands of years. Links with the past are obvious in the shape of the many monuments which are to be found all over the city, flanked by buildings of our own time. The large number of Christian churches gives the city a predominantly Byzantine character, and if Athens gives the visitor the impression of contact with the ancient Greek religion, in Thessaloniki it is undoubtedly Christianity which makes its presence most strongly felt.

It was without dispute St Paul who cul-

tivated the first seeds of the new religion in Thessaloniki. It seems that his preaching drew a response on his very first visit in 49 AD. His first concern on arriving in the city was to make contact with the local Jewish synagogue: "Following his usual practice Paul went to their meeting; and for the next three Sabbaths he argued with them, quoting texts of scripture which he expounded and applied to show that the Messiah had to suffer and rise from the dead. 'And this Jesus', he said, 'Whom I am proclaiming to you is the Messiah.' Some of them were convinced and joined Paul and Silas, as did a great number of godfearing Gentiles and a good many influential women" (Acts 17, 2 - 4).

According to the Acts of the Apostles, Paul stayed in Thessaloniki three weeks. However, there is a passage in the first letter which he sent to the Thessalonians which suggests that his stay was of longer duration: "You remember, my friends, our toil and drudgery; night and day we

city the synagogue was situated in Paul's time. A large variety of views as to its exact location has been expressed by scholars and travellers, some placing it in the vicinity of the Church of St Demetrius, others near Aghia Sophia, and others near the Vlatades Monastery. All these views are, however, no more than hypotheses, since none of them has received confirmation from archaeology. Paul must, anyway, have preached in other parts of the city for so many Greeks to have been converted.

Much light is thrown on the content of Paul's preaching in Thessaloniki by the Acts of the Apostles and the two letters to the Thessalonians. According to these sources, his central themes were the Passion and Resurrection of Christ and His Second Coming. Paul urged the Christians to be vigilant and to observe God's law, since when the Day of Judgment came, they would have to give an account of themselves before Christ, the just judge. It would seem that this preaching greatly disturbed the inhabitants and for this reason Paul had to stress that the hour of judgment would come only after the appearance of the Antichrist (II Thess. 2, 3 -5).

As can be seen from the epistles, there were many converts to Christianity in Thessaloniki. Paul never ceased to com-

worked for a living, rather than be a burden to any of you while we proclaimed to you the good news of God" (I Thess. 2, 9). The fact that Paul needed to work suggests that he stayed for some time -probably longer than three weeks. Moreover, the Epistle to the Philipppians states that while Paul was at Thessaloniki aid was sent to him twice (Phil. 4, 16). This would hardly have been possible, or even necessary, in the space of three weeks.

We do not know whereabouts in the

78-79. Thessaloniki, part of the Byzantine walls of the town with the Trigonion Tower

mend the city's Christian community for its faith and its constant fortitude: "You, in turn, followed the example set by us and by the Lord; the welcome you gave the message meant grave suffering for you, yet you rejoiced in the Holy Spirit; and so you have become a model for all believers in Macedonia and in Achaia. From you the word of the Lord rang out; and not in Macedonia and Achaia alone, but everywhere your faith in God has become common knowledge" (I Thess. 1, 6 - 9).

Nevertheless, Paul's visit to Thessaloniki involved him yet again in persecution. "The Jews in their jealousy recruited some ruffians from the dregs of society to gather a mob. They put the city in an uproar, and made for Jason's house with the intention of bringing Paul and Silas before the town assembly. Failing to find them, they dragged Jason himself and some members of the congregation before the magistrates, shouting, 'The men who have made trouble the whole world over have now come here, and Jason has harboured them. All of them flout the emperor's laws, and assert there is a rival

king, Jesus.' These words alarmed the mob and the magistrates also, who took security from Jason and the others before letting them go" (Acts 17, 5 - 9). The charges made by the Jews against Paul and Silas were similar to the accusations against them at Philippi. Nor is it any coincidence that Christ Himself was arrested and crucified because He was considered a danger to the integrity of the Roman state. In Thessaloniki, Paul and Silas managed to escape arrest by leaving Jason's house and the city secretly. According to tradition, the house where they stayed was in the Upper City, near the spot where the Vlatades Monastery was later built. However, this story has never received any confirmation, although it is true that a district very close to the Monastery bears to this day the name of 'Aghios Pavlos' (St Paul). There are two churches nearby dedicated to him, a small one built in the late nineteenth century and a larger one dating from 1950. It is maintained, without any proof, that it was to the site of the older church that Paul fled after leaving the house of Jason.

When Paul had finished his visits to the cities of Macedonia and had travelled to southern Greece as far as Athens, he sent Timothy to Thessaloniki to obtain information on the progress of the church there. Timothy, having carried out this commission, returned and met up with Paul in Corinth in 50/51 BC. It was then that, with a space of a few weeks between them, the two letters to the Thessalonians, the earliest texts in the New Testament, were written. Their purpose was to encourage the Christians in their difficulties, since they continued to be persecuted by the Jews. Paul, in fact, wished to return to Thessaloniki, but was unable to put this desire into immediate effect. "My friends, when for a short spell you were lost to us -out of sight but not out of mind - we were exceedingly anxious to see you again. So we made up our minds to visit you- I, Paul, more than once- but Satan thwarted us. For what hope or joy or triumphal crown is there for us when we stand before our Lord Jesus at His coming? What indeed but you? You are our glory and our joy" (I Thess. 2, 17 - 20). It was only during the course of his third journey (52 - 56 BC) that, in all probability, he was able to revisit for a second and third time the city for which he had such an affection, when, from Ephesus, he again toured the new Christian churches and then retraced his steps to return to Asia Minor.

80. Thessaloniki, the Church of St Catherine, 1330-1340 AD

81. Thessaloniki, view of the town and part of the Byzantine fortifications

VERIA (BEREA)

L eaving Thessaloniki by night, Paul and Silas headed south-west, arriving, after some 70 kilometres, at Berea, the modern Veria. Veria stands in the foothills of Mt Vermio on a plateau which is crossed by the River Tripota-mos, a tributary of the Aliacmon. It is to the waterfalls on this river that the city owes the industrial development which it has to show today, when it also makes its living from commerce, farming and stockbreeding. Veria is not on the main tourist routes, but that does not mean that it is lacking in beauty and picturesqueness. Its modern face is soon lost sight of in the older districts of the town with their narrow cobbled alleys and the traditional houses. Among these, its numerous Byzantine churches, of exceptional interest, are a reminder of past glories. Veria's history can be traced in the galleries of its Archaeological Museum.

The Veria area has been inhabited from at least the sixth millennium BC. At a short distance from the city, a Neolithic settlement has been excavated at Nea Niko-mideia. The houses which have been found have a square ground plan and were built with beams, tree branches and clay. The city itself is mentioned by name for the first time by Thucydides. In mythology, it was founded by Berea, daughter of Ocean and of Thetis. Its original inhabitants were tribesmen from Thrace, but these were defeat-ed by the Macedonians and handed over their city to them. Archaeology has brought to light evidence for the city's history from the fourth century BC. To that period be-longs an extensive cemetery and parts of a stadium and of the ancient market-place. Veria was taken by the Romans in 168 BC and soon afterwards became one of the most important cities of Macedonia.

It was equally important during the Byzantine period, as can be seen from the fact that no fewer than 48 churches of that time have survived. From the early eleventh century Veria was a distinct administrative region of Macedonia. Between the years 1070 and 1080, the Old Cathedral, a wooden-roofed, three-aisled basilica -decorated with wall-paintings of the twelfth to the fourteenth century- was constructed. From 1204 to 1215/6 the city was occupied by the Latins and it was then taken by Theodore Angelus, Despot of Epirus, before being annexed to the Empire of Nicaea in 1246. In the time of Andronicus II Palaeologus, the Church of the Resurrection of Christ, or of Christ as it is called today, was begun (1315). This is a small single-aisled church, decorated by the important fourteenth-century artist Georgios Kallierghis. From 1343 until it was taken by the Turks in 1387, Veria was ruled alternately by Ioannis and Manuel Cantacuzenus and the Kral of the Serbians, Dushan. Christian churches continued to be built throughout the centuries of Turkish rule, typical examples being Our Lady 'Haviara', Our Lady 'Kyriotissa' (fifteenth century) and St Nicholas (sixteenth century). The city was finally liberated from the Turks in 1912,

after the Balkan Wars.

The very large number of churches with which Veria has been adorned through the ages testifies to the existence of a long Christian tradition, the origins of which are undoubtedly to be sought in St Paul's visit. When they arrived here, Paul and Silas immediately made for the Jewish synagogue, where they met Timothy, from whom they had separated at Philippi. Their preaching most have met with a considerable response from the people of Veria, both Jews and Gentiles. "The Jews here

were more fair-minded than those at Thessolonica: they received the message with great eagerness, studying the scriptures every day to see whether it was true. Many of them therefore became believers, and so did a fair number of gentiles, women of standing as well as men" (Acts 17, 11 - 12). It is not known where Paul taught, but a shrine, with a representation of him in mosaic, has been dedicated to his memory in the south-eastern part of the town. Local tradition holds that the message of Christianity was first delivered from the hill on this spot.

Paul stayed for some time in Veria, but was forced to leave after more persecution, organised by the Jews of Thessaloniki: "But when the Thessalonian Jews learnt that the word of God had been proclaimed by Paul in Berea, they followed him there to stir up trouble and rouse the rabble. At once the members of the congregation sent Paul down to the coast, while Silas and Timothy both stayed behind" (Acts 17, 13 - 14).

82. Veria, Apostle Paul, mosaic from the shrine which stands today at the spot where, according to tradition, Paul taught

84. (above) Veria, the "Tribune" (Bema) of Apostle Paul, the spot where, according to tradition, Paul taught

84. (below) Veria, the Old Cathedral, 1070-1080 AD

85. (above) Veria, view of the old Jewish quarter of the town, with a restored Synagogue on the left

DION

Although it is nowhere stated that Paul passed through the city of Dion, many scholars suppose that it would have been from there that the vessel taking him to his next recorded destination, Athens, set out. This is extremely probable, given that Dion was the nearest port to Veria. The archaeological site of Dion is today six kilometres from the sea, but this is the result of the silting up which has occurred in the course of the centuries.

Dion was a city of great importance for the ancient Macedonians and was a Panhellenic religious centre. Standing between Olympus, the home of the gods, and the Pierian Mountains, the dwelling-place of the Muses, it developed cults linked with these deities at an early date. In the late fifth century BC, Archelaus, King of Macedonia, inaugurated in this area the Olympia, a festival dedicated to Zeus and the Muses. The Olympia lasted nine days - one day for each Muse- and included musical and athletic competitions. According to the ancient sources, before Alexander the Great embarked upon his cam-

paign, he took part in this festival and paid the appropriate tribute to Zeus. The goddess Demeter was also worshipped at Dion; her sanctuary is one of the most ancient in Macedonia, dating from around 500 BC. Archaeological digs have also brought to light two other sanctuaries, dedicated to Isis and Asclepius respectively, a Hellenistic theatre and another dating from Roman times, a complex of luxurious Roman baths, decorated with statues of the family of Asclepius and with mosaics, sections of the city walls (late fourth century BC to the Roman period), a large house with mosaic floors of around 200 AD, and three early Christian basilicas. The movable finds are housed in the local archaeological museum. Dion was taken by the Romans in 168 BC and became a Roman colony under the name of Colonia Julia Diensis. The life of the city came to an end in the fifth century AD, when its houses and sanctuaries were destroyed by barbarians.

86-87. Dion, views from the archaeological site

ATHENS

"Paul's escort brought him as far as Athens, and came away with
instructions for Silas and Timothy to rejoin him with all speed"
(Acts 17, 15).

After Macedonia, Paul chose to preach Christianity in Athens, the cradle of
the ancient Greek religion. The prestige of the city of the intellect and of
art was still such that if his preaching were accepted by its citizens, it could
then be disseminated throughout the civilised world. Nor would it be fan-
ciful to suppose that the Apostle of the Gentiles was himself curious to see the centre
of a culture which he had learnt so much about at Tarsus.

When Paul visited it in 49/50 AD, Athens was already a city with thousands of
years of history. Its first inhabitants established themselves in the area of the Acropolis
in the Neolithic period, while the first Hellenes arrived in around 2000 BC. During
the Mycenaean period (sixteenth to the twelfth centuries BC), the hill of the Acropolis
was fortified for the security of the settlement and of the royal palace. According to
tradition, Theseus, the most important of the kings of Athens, created a unified city-
state with Athens as its centre by amalgamating the settlements of Attica. This unifica-
tion ('synoecism') must have taken place in the eighth century BC and gave a major
boost to the development of Athens. In the seventh century, the power of the monarch
passed into the hands of the aristocrats, while in 624 BC the law was codified for the
first time by Draco. In 594 BC, the Athenians empowered Solon, one of the 'Seven
Sages' of antiquity, to draw up new laws. His reforms gave the Athenian state a pluto-
cratic character, since the offices and obligations of citizens were determined on the
basis of their income. In 561/560 BC, Pisistratus, with the help of the lower classes of
society, established a tyranny at Athens; this was maintained by his sons Hipparchus
and Hippias until 510 BC. During the course of the tyranny the city was adorned
with a large number of monuments and sanctuaries, while at the same period the
Homeric epics were set down in writing, the great festival of the Panathenaea was re-

organised, and the worship of Dionysus, the cult from which the theatre grew, introduced. Following reforms proposed by Cleisthenes in 508 BC, a democratic political system was introduced.

Between 490 and 480/479 BC, the citizens of Athens played a leading role in the resistance to the Persians, who wished to expand into Greek territory. In the course of the Persian Wars, Athens was burnt twice; it was subsequently rebuilt and fortified on the initiative of Themistocles, who was also responsible for the building up of the city's naval strength and the foundation of the so-called Delian League in 478 BC. The League, of which a large number of Greek cities were members, had as its initial purpose to counter the Persian threat by joint action. Within it, Athens acquired a leading role and soon emerged as the first

into two opposing camps, the chief rivals being Athens and Sparta, the second most important city of Greece. In 404 BC, Athens was finally defeated, and from that point on its decline began. In 338 BC it was taken by Philip II of Macedonia, who nevertheless respected its culture, as did his son Alexander. In the Hellenistic period it was dependent upon the policies of Alexander's successors. In the second century BC it fell into the hands of the Romans. In 86 BC Athens was looted by the Roman consul Sulla, an experience from which it took many years to recover.

Athens in the time of the Apostle Paul was not, of course, the flourishing city of the Classical period, but it still retained some measure of the glory of the past and its numerous monuments, witnesses to its supremacy in the arts and sciences. Most of these monuments can be seen today, thanks to the excavations which have been carried out untiringly all over the city. Undoubtedly, in the first century AD even more of them would have been standing in their original positions and Paul would have visited them or seen them in the course of his visit. The Acts of the Apostles tells us: "While Paul was waiting for them at Athens, he was outraged to see the city so full of idols. He argued in the synagogue with the Jews and gentile worshippers, and also in the city square every day with casual passers-by" (Acts 17, 16 - 17).

No doubt Paul's first acquaintance with

city of Greece. At the same time, Pericles, the creator of the 'Golden Age', the most brilliant period of Athenian history, had become the city's political leader. In his time, democracy reached its most mature expression and in every field of intellectual activity and the arts it was an age of greatness and glory. None of this, however, could avert the Peloponnesian War, which broke out in 431 BC and divided Greece

89. Athens, view of the town, with the Odeon of Herod Atticus (2nd century AD) and the Acropolis

90. Athens, the Parthenon on the Acropolis, 447-432 BC

the works of the Athenians had already been made during the course of his voyage. From Dion, Paul's ship would have taken him down the Thermaic Gulf and along the coast of Euboea and would then have turned west, thus bringing him to Cape Sounion in Attica. Here Paul would have seen the imposing Temple of Poseidon, which even today impresses visitors approaching Athens by sea. On the Sounion promontory Poseidon and Athena, the two deities who competed to become protector of Athens, Poseidon providing a wild horse and Athena an olive branch, were worshipped in two separate sanctuaries. The Athenians chose the gift of Athena and gave her name to their city, but they also worshipped Poseidon, the god of the sea, at the end of a promontory which domi-

nates a wide expanse of sea. The temple which Paul would have seen was of marble, of the Doric order, and had been built in the age of Pericles. The Ionic Temple of Athena had already been destroyed in Sulla's raid. Around Sounion's rock there would also have been visible some sections of the wall which the Athenians built in 412 BC, during the Peloponnesian War, since Sounion, apart from being a place of worship, was a fortress of strategic importance. Tradition tells us that travellers approaching by sea could also see from a great distance the famous statue of Athena Promachus, the work of the great Athenian

92. Attica, the Temple of Poseidon at Sounion, 444-440 BC

93. Athens, view of the Street of the Tombs in the ancient Kerameikos Cemetery

sculptor Phidias, which was set up on the Acropolis to commemorate the victory over the Persians at the Battle of Marathon in 490 BC.

After turning to the north, Paul's ship would, after passing close to the islands of Aegina and Salamis in the Saronic Gulf, have reached Piraeus. Today Greece's biggest port, Piraeus was developed in the time of Themistocles, when Athens was beginning to depend upon her naval power. The city was built according to the Hippodamian system and was fortified, soon coming to serve as the port of Athens. In 478 BC, the road linking the two cities was fortified by means of the so-called Long Walls and thus communication between the two became more secure. In the time of Paul, however, Piraeus was in de-

cline and its buildings had been destroyed as a result of Sulla's raid in 86 BC. Testimony to this is provided not only by archaeological research but by another Roman, Pausanias, who in the second century AD visited many Greek cities and left a detailed description of the monuments which he saw in the course of his travels. Paul's approach to Athens can be reconstructed on the basis of the route followed by Pausanias, since only a century separated the two visitors.

In order to reach Athens from Piraeus, he would have gone in a north-easterly direction, with the Parthenon on the hill of the Acropolis before him to guide him. The Acropolis was the place where the worship of Athena, the city's most important deity developed. Originally it had been an inhabited area, but in the sixth century BC, when Pisistratus built a limestone temple to Athena, it had already taken on religious significance. It was in honour of the city's patron deity that the Panathenaea festival, which included athletic competitions and a magnificent procession of all the citizens, was held. The purpose of the Panathenaea procession was the presentation to the statue of Athena of a new garment ('peplos'). This was accompanied by sacrifices on the Acropolis. The Panathenaea festival was at its most magnificent in the fifth century BC, when the Sacred Rock was adorned with buildings of great splendour. In 437 - 432 BC, the monumental Propylaea was built by the architect Mnesicles at the western entrance to the Acropolis, together with the Ionic Temple of Athena Nike, to commemorate the victory over the Persians.

The Parthenon, the symbol of democratic Athens, was completed between 447 and 432 BC, to plans by the architects Ictinus and Callicrates. It was a peripteral Doric temple with Ionic features, built in Pentelic marble and decorated with the pioneering sculptures of Phidias. Also the work of Phidias was the famous Ionic frieze, showing the Panathenaic procession, and the chryselephantine (gold and ivory) statue of Athena in the interior of the temple. The Temple of Athena Parthenos, thanks to the refinements and curvatures of its surfaces, gives the impression more of a work of sculpture than of ordinary architecture.

In 421 - 406 BC, the Erechtheum was constructed to the north of the Parthenon. This was an Ionic temple of original design, dedicated to the deities associated with the past of the city. On its southern facade stood the Caryatids, statues of 'Korai' serving as supports and lending beauty and grace to the building. The space between the various buildings was occupied by numerous statues, votive offerings of the faithful. On the southern slopes of the Acropolis was the sanctuary of Dionysus with its theatre, the place in which the works of the great dramatists of antiquity were staged for the first time. In Paul's time, the Theatre of Dionysus had been badly damaged by Sulla and must have been undergoing repair. The famous Odeion of Pericles, next to the Theatre of Dionysus, had suffered the same fate, but by Paul's time had already been rebuilt. In the same area, the sanctuary of the healer-god Asclepius, dating from the late fifth century BC, and the stoa (colonnade) built by the King of Pergamum Eumenes II in the second century BC could also be seen. The Theatre of Herod Atticus, which lives on thanks to its use every summer in the Athens Festival, had not yet been built (it was completed in the second century AD). We are not told anywhere that Paul visited

94. Athens, the Roman Agora, 1st century BC. On the right the mosque Fetiche, 16th century AD

95. Athens, the Temple of Hephaestus on the site of the ancient Agora, 450-421/415 BC.

the Acropolis, but he can hardly have avoided seeing its monuments, since the Sacred Rock dominated the centre of the city.

The sight of the walls laid waste by Sulla as one approached Athens would have been very striking. We do not know by which gate Paul entered the city, but it is most likely that he passed through the most central entrance, on the north-western side, the site of the Sacred Gate and the Dipylon. In this area, the Kerameikos,

there was a cemetery with the tombs of private citizens and of the war dead. This was an imposing site at all the periods when it was in use, since the funerary monuments were surmounted with statues and columns of superb workmanship.

From the Dipylon Gate a main street, known as the 'Dromos', led to the Agora of Athens, where it changed its name to the Panathenaic Way and led up to the Acropolis. The Agora was the political, administrative, commercial and religious centre of the city.

The Acts of the Apostles renders it certain that Paul visited the Agora - and was enraged by the sight of the fine buildings and statues of the ancient Greek religion. On its western side would certainly have seen the Stoa Basileios (sixth century BC), headquarters of the magistrate known as the Archon-Basileus, the Stoa (colonnade) of Zeus (fifth century BC) and the statue of Zeus, the Ionic Temple of Apollo Patroös and the statue of Apollo, the work of the sculptor Euphranor (fourth century BC), the Metroon -for the worship of the mother of the gods, Rhea-Cybele, and for the keeping of the state archives - of the second century BC, the Bouleuterion (Council House) late fifth century BC, and the circular Tholos (fifth century BC), a building with an administrative and, in all probability, religious function. Paul could hardly have avoided seeing the monumental Temple of Hephaestus and of Athena Ergane (patrons of craftsmen), built in the mid fifth century BC on the Colonos Agoraios hill. This was a Doric peripteral tem-

ple, decorated with fine sculptures of mythological scenes. Inside it had statues of the deities to which it was dedicated, the work of the sculptor Alcamenes. In the triangular 'piazza' of the Agora was the Peribolos (precinct) of the Eponymous Heroes,

96. (above) Athens, the Theatre of Dionysus (4th century BC), as it was reconstructed at the Roman period

96. (below) Athens, the Propylaea (437-432 BC) and the Ionic Temple of Athena Nike (427-424 BC) on the Acropolis

97. Athens, the Ionic Temple of Erechtheus (Erectheum) on the Acropolis, 421-414 BC

with statues of the heroes who had given their names to the tribes of Attica (mid fourth century BC), a Doric temple dedicated to the god Ares (fifth century BC), an altar for the worship of the Twelve Gods (522/1 BC), and the Odeion, built by Augustus's son-in-law Agrippa. Among the statues which stood in the open spaces, the group showing Peace and Prosperity, the work of the sculptor Cephisodotus (fourth century BC) and the two showing Harmodius and Aristogeiton, who in 514 BC

slew the tyrant Hipparchus, stood out. The older of the two groups (sixth century BC) was carved by Antenor and the later one by Critias and Nesiotes (early fifth century BC). The southern side of the Agora was occupied by two colonnades of the second century BC, the Heliaea building, from the sixth century BC, the most important law court of Athens, and the Enneakrounos fountain, of the time of Pisistratus. On the east, the Agora was dominated by the Stoa of Attalus, built in 150 BC by Attalus II, King of Pergamum, and used today as the Agora Museum. In front of this colonnade was a rostrum for public speakers and a bronze statue of Attalus II.

The most southerly building in the Agora was the Stoa Poikile, or painted portico, the foundations of which survive to-day, outside the fenced archaeological site. This was built around 460 BC and was decorated with works of the best painters of the age, such as Polygnotus and Panaenus. From the third century BC, this stoa was where the followers of the philosopher Zeno met, thus acquiring the name of 'Stoics'. The Acts of the Apostles tells us that Paul spoke with the philosophers of Athens and it is reasonable to suppose that such conversations would have taken place in the Stoa Poikile. "Moreover, some of the Epicurean and Stoic philosophers joined issue with him. Some said, 'What can this charlatan be trying to say?' and others, 'He appears to be a propagandist for foreign deities' -this because he was preaching about Jesus and the Resurrection" (Acts 17, 18).

Although it would seem that at first the Athenians did not understand what Paul was telling them, they were, nevertheless, willing to listen with interest to the arguments on which he based his claims. "They brought him to the ... Areopagus and asked, May we know what this new doctrine is that you propound? You are introducing ideas that sound strange to us, and we should like to know what they mean.' Now, all the Athenians and the resident

98. (left) Athens, part of the Temple of Hephaestus. In the background: the Acropoli

98. (right) Athens, the water-clock of Andronicus Kyrrhestes, known as the Tower of the Winds, 1st century AD

99. Athens, the Stoa (Colonnade) of Attalus II (159-138 BC) in the ancient Agora, used today as the Agora Museum

foreigners had time for nothing except talking or hearing about the latest novelty" (Acts 17, 19 - 21). Athens was the city where, in the past, philosophy and rhetoric had risen to their greatest heights and the need of its citizens to be kept informed of the latest theories and to subject them to examination lived on even when its greatest glory was in the past. Thus they led Paul to the Areopagus, where he could explain his preaching in greater detail. The Areopagus is a rocky hill to the west of the Acropolis, so-called either because there, according to tradition, the god Ares was tried, or because it was the site of the sanctuary of the Arai - Erinyes, or Furies -deities who took vengeance on murderers. In the seventh century BC, the name of Areopagus was taken by a political body with administrative and judicial duties, but whose powers in the fifth century were restricted to trying cases of murder. The text of the Acts of the Apostles does not make it clear whether Paul was taken to Areopagus hill or to the judicial body of the same name, who could have met somewhere else in the city. The prevailing view is that Paul's address was given on the Areopagus hill -the 'Hill of Mars'. It is there on 29 June each year, the Feast of St Peter and St Paul, that a service is held in their honour.

The authenticity of Paul's speech, as recorded in the Acts of the Apostles, has been questioned by a considerable number of scholars. They maintain that such an address was not the product of Paul's thinking, but rather of that of Luke himself, with his greater familiarity with Greek culture. This view is based upon the fact that

Paul's famous speech to the Athenians is imbued with ideas derived from Greek theories of the cosmos. However, Paul was well enough acquainted with the philosophy of the Greeks to have used it in order to make himself more intelligible. According to the Acts of the Apostles: "Paul stood up before the ... Areopagus and began: 'Men of Athens, I see that in everything that concerns religion you are uncommonly scrupulous. As I was looking at the objects of your worship, I noticed among other things an altar bearing the inscription "To an unknown God". What you worship but do not know - this is what I now proclaim. The God who created the world and everything in it, and who is Lord of heaven and earth, does not live in shrines made by human hands. It is not because He lacks anything that He accepts service at our hands, for He is Himself the universal giver of life and breath -indeed of everything. He created from one stock every nation of men to inhabit the whole earth's surface. He determined the eras of history and the limits of their territory. They were to seek God in the hope that, groping after him, they might find Him; though indeed He is not far from each one of us, for in Him we live and move, in Him we exist; as some of your own poets have said, "We are also his offspring." Being God's offspring, then, we ought not to suppose that the deity is like an image in gold or silver or stone, shaped by human craftsmanship and design. God has overlooked the age of ignorance; but now he commands men and women everywhere to repent, because He has fixed the day on which He will have the world judged, and justly judged, by a man whom He has designated; of this He has given assurance to all by raising him from the dead.' When they heard about the raising of the dead, some scoffed; others said, 'We will hear you on this subject some other time.' So Paul left the assembly. Some men joined him and became believers, including Dionysius, a member of the Council of the Areopagus; and also a woman named Damaris, with others besides" (Acts 17, 22 - 34).

The altar of the Unknown God to which Paul refers has not been discovered in archaeological digs in Athens. Nevertheless, Pausanias in his travel writings tells us that on his way from Piraeus he encountered altars dedicated to the Unknown Gods. The worship in late antiquity of unknown deities or of all the deities together is known to us from the historical sources. This was due chiefly to superstition and the fear lest any god or goddess should be left out. A kind of parallel could be drawn with the observance in the Christian Church of All Saints' Day.

The preaching of Paul does not seem to have met with the same response in Athens as it did in other large cities of Greece. The Athenians adopted an attitude of scepticism towards him, particularly when he spoke of the resurrection of the dead, whereas Paul regarded it as a weakness of Greek thought

101. (above) the Areopagus Hill (Hill of Mars), where Paul's address was given

101. (below) Athens, general view of the ancient Agora

that it was unable to comprehend the message of resurrection contained in Christianity. On the other hand, the whole of Greek philosophy was based on argumentation and irrefutable, palpable proofs. Nonetheless, although the Athenians were unable to agree with Paul's views, they do not seem to have persecuted or arrested him, as was the case in other places. The number of those who accepted Christianity was exceptionally small: the Acts of the Apostles names Damaris, of whom nothing else is known, and Dionysius the Areopagite, who, tradition maintains, became bishop of the city and died a martyr's death under Diocletian at the end of the first century. This suggests the existence of a Christian community at Athens, certainly linked with Paul's visit, but there is no evidence for anything of the kind either in the Acts of the Apostles or in the epistles. Dionysius the Areopagite is today honoured as the patron saint of Athens. His feast day is 3 October, while a church dedicated to him stands in the centre of the city (Skoufa St), decorated with mosaics showing Paul addressing the Athenians.

According to the view generally held today, a good many years had to pass before the Christian religion became accepted in Athens. In the second century AD the city enjoyed a 'second spring', thanks to the favour shown towards it by the Emperor Hadrian. To him it owed its expansion beyond its old boundaries and the building

of a large number of magnificent buildings, such as the Temple of Olympian Zeus
in the area of the Ilissus river, a fine library
near the ancient and the Roman Agora, an
aqueduct, and a Nymphaion, a building
around a fountain where the Nymphs were
worshipped. Nevertheless, the ancient
sources mention the names of certain
Athenian Christians of the second century,
including one Aristides, who attempted to
speak to the Emperor Hadrian himself
about the new religion. In the end, the ancient Greek religion was dealt a mortal
blow when in the fifth century the Emper-
or Theodosius II forbade heathen worship
and when, in 529 AD, Justinian closed the
city's schools of philosophy.

*102. Athens, the Church of Our Lady "Gorgoepikoos"
or St Eleutherios, 12th century BC*

*103. (above) Athens, the church in the Monastery of
Kaisariani, late 11th century AD*

*103. (below) Athens, the Church of the Holy Apostles
on the site of the ancient Agora, late 10th century AD*

With the triumph of Christianity, many of the ancient temples of Athens were converted into Christian churches. The Parthenon and the Erechtheum took on the form of Christian basilicas in the sixth century, the Temple of Hephaestus in the ancient Agora was consecrated in the seventh century to St George, and two basilicas were built in the Theatre of Dionysus and the sanctuary of Asclepius respectively, in the fifth century, with the appropriate adaptation of the existing buildings. At the same period new churches of the basilica type were built. These included the basilica on the Ilissus, dedicated to St Leonidis (fifth - sixth century), the Basilica of St Nicholas very near it, and the basilica of Anchesmos, behind the present-day Church of St Dionysius the Areopagite. After a period of decline, Byzantine art in Athens reached its zenith in the Middle Byzantine period (843 - 1204). It was then that a large number of churches, the majority of which have survived, was built. Their chief characteristic was the so-called Athenian dome with its slender proportions and the austerity of its external surfaces. Almost all the Athenian churches belong to the cross-in-square type, predominant at that time. Of particular interest are the Church of St Nicholas Rangavas in the Plaka district (1031 - 1050), the Kapnikarea (mid eleventh century), the Church of Sts Theodore (1065), the katholikon (main church) of the Kaisariani Monastery (late eleventh century), Our Lady 'Gorgoepikoös' (twelfth century), which serves as a chapel to Athens Cathedral, and the Church of the Holy Apostles, built around 1000 on the site of the ancient Agora in its own individual four-apse architectural style. Belonging to the octagonal type is the Church of Soteira Lykodimou (the Russian Church) and the katholikon of the Dafni Monastery (late eleventh century), of particular importance for its mosaic decoration.

Following the fall of Constantinople to the Franks in 1204, Athens fell into the hands of Otto de la Roche of Burgundy, while from the fourteenth century it was held successively by the Catalans, the Florentine Acciaiuoli family, the Venetians and the Byzantines. In 1458 it fell to the Turks and the Acropolis became a Turkish village. In 1687, during the Venetian-Turkish War, it was bombarded and captured by the Venetian Morosini. In 1690 it was recovered by the Turks, finally achieving its liberation in 1833 and becoming the capital of the new Greek state. At that period the city was built afresh to the plans of the architects Kleanthis and Schaubert, most of the buildings following the nineteenth-century neo-Classical style. Many of these buildings survive today, giving their own particular flavour to the

modern megalopolis. Athens today, with a population of five million, is Greece's capital not only geographically, but in every field of activity.

104. Attica, Christ Pantocrator, mosaic from the Monastery of Daphni, about 1100 AD

105. (above) Athens, the Temple of Olympian Zeus, 6th century BC – 2nd century AD

105. (below) Athens, the Choregic Monument of Lysicrates, devoted by the sponsor (choregos) of a theatrical play which won in the Drama Contests of 334 BC.

CORINTH

"After this he left Athens and went to Corinth" (Acts 18, 1).

I t is not known whether Paul travelled to Corinth by land or sea. If by sea, the vessel would have crossed the Saronic Gulf and anchored at the port of Cenchreae, approximately nine kilometres south of Corinth. The route by land would have differed little from that followed today: leaving Athens, Paul would have passed through the Sacred Gate in the Kerameikos area and would have followed the Sacred Way, leading to Eleusis. He would then have passed through the Megarid, with the coast of the island of Salamis to the south, and following a route parallel with the Saronic Gulf, he would have arrived at the Isthmus of Corinth, on the boundary of the Peloponnese. Today it is the Corinth Canal which divides the Prefecture of Attica from that of Corinthia.

In Paul's time, of course, the Corinth Canal had yet to be dug, although such an enterprise had in the past frequently been decided upon by the various tyrants of the city. In fact, in 67 AD, on the decision of the Emperor Nero, work was started in cutting through the isthmus, but it was never completed. It was only in 1893 that  this major project was carried out and a six-kilometre canal linked the Gulf of Corinth with the Saronic Gulf. In ancient times the problem of crossing the isthmus was solved in another way: the tyrants of Corinth had constructed a paved road, the so-called Diolkos, on which vessels were drawn on a wheeled vehicle from the one gulf to the other. This

106. Corinth, Byzantine capital
107. Corinth, the Temple of Apollo, about 540 BC

arrangement was of immense importance for a rich commercial city such as Corinth.

The Corinth area was first inhabited in the Neolithic period, in the fourth millennium BC. Settlement in the area was favoured by a plentiful water supply and the natural environment: there was to the south the rock of the Acrocorinth, a natural stronghold which served as the citadel of the city, while to the east and south there were the ports of Lechaion and Cenchreae, which played an important part in Corinth's development. Furthermore, the isthmus, the sole link between the Peloponnese and the rest of Greece, was nearby. In prehistoric times, Corinth was one of the richest cities in Greece. Its first king in historical times

was said to have been Aletes, leader of the Dorians, who arrived in the region around 1000 BC. In the eighth century BC, the Corinthians founded the colonies of Corcyra (today's Corfu) and Syracuse in Sicily and developed into the leading maritime power of Greece. In 657 BC, Cypselus, with the aid of the poorer classes, established a tyranny at Corinth. Cypselus and his son Periander - one of the Seven Sages of antiquity - founded other colonies and were patrons of the arts and sciences. It was in the time of the

108. Corinth, Diolkos, a paved road on which vessels were drawn on a wheeled vehicle from the Saronic Gulf to the Gulf of Corinth and vice versa

109. Corinth, the Corinth Canal, dug in 1893

Cypselids that the Isthmian Games were re-organised and soon acquired a Panhellenic character. These were held every two years at the sanctuary of Poseidon at Isthmia, east of Corinth, and included athlet-

ic contests and religious ceremonies. The foundations of the Doric Temple of Poseidon, initially built in the seventh century BC, of a theatre, of two stadiums, of the Classical and of the Hellenistic periods, and of a circular temple dedicated to Palaemon-Melicertes, the mythical figure in whose memory the Games were said to have been inaugurated, survive on the archaeological site.

In 580 BC the Spartans ended the Cypselid tyranny and gave their support to an aristocratic regime. At that point the city became Sparta's ally and one of the strongest members of the Peloponnesian alliance. Around 540 BC the Doric Temple of Apollo, which today dominates the archaeological site of Corinth, was built.

During the Persian Wars, Corinth took part in almost all the battles. At a later date, in order to counter the growing power of Athens, it was one of the leading instigators of the Peloponnesian War (431 - 404 BC). By the end of the War, however, in spite of being on the side of victorious Sparta, it had lost its leading place in Greek affairs. In 338 BC it was taken by Philip II, who, the same year, was crowned king and commander-in-chief of the Hellenes at the Isthmus. It was there too that Alexander the Great convened a Panhellenic conference and succeeded in becoming leader of the campaign against the Persians. In 243 BC, the city joined the Achaean League and later became its capital, but the Achaean forces were defeated by the Romans in 146 BC, when

110. (above) Corinth, the monumental Peirene fountain, 2nd century BC

110. (below) Corinth, the Roman Northwest shops

111. (above) Corinth, view of the Roman Agora. In the background: the Temple of Apollo, about 540 BC

111. (below) Corinth, the Roman Temple of Octavia, sister of Augustus

the Roman general Mummius laid Corinth waste, after which it remained in ruins for a whole century. It was Julius Caesar who rebuilt it in 46 BC, making it a colony of veterans with the name of Colonia Julia Corinthiensis. The new city developed rapidly and by the time of Paul's visit in 50/51 AD had become the capital of the Roman province of Achaea. In the second century AD it was adorned with buildings of great splendour, thanks to the generosity of the Emperor Hadrian and of Herodes Atticus. The archaeological site

112. (above) Corinth, Byzantine bas-relief

112. (below) Corinth, view from the archeological site. In the background: the Acrocorinth

113. Corinth, the "Tribune" (Bema) of Gallio, the court where Paul was brought during his visit in the town

of Corinth today preserves the remains of the buildings of the Roman forum, many of which Paul would have seen. These include the Temple of Octavia, sister of Augustus, a series of miniature temples, standing on an elevated base, a large number of shops, the Julian Basilica, of the period of Augustus, the monumental Peirene fountain, the gift of Herodes Atticus, the northern basilica, its facade decorated with colossal figures of barbarians, an Odeion and a theatre, its initial phase dating from the fourth century BC. Naturally, St Paul would not have missed the imposing Temple of Apollo.

In the Byzantine period, Corinth was frequently raided, first by the Goths, who looted the city in 267 and 395 BC. The mid fifth century saw the building of an important Christian monument a little way outside Corinth, the so-called Basilica of Lechaion, dedicated to St Leonidis and the women who were martyred with him. In the next century, the Emperor Justinian fortified the general area, constructing

the famous Isthmian Wall or Hexamilion, of a length of 7,300 metres. In the Middle Ages, the Acrocorinth played an important role in the defence of the city. Nevertheless, between then and the nineteenth century, Corinth had a number of conquerors: Normans, Franks, Venetians, and Turks (1458). After the War of Independence of 1821 against the Turks, the city was liberated and was an unsuccessful candidate for the role of capital of the newly-constituted Greek state. In 1858, a major earthquake destroyed the small village which stood on the site of ancient Corinth, and a new city was built closer to the Isthmus, to be rebuilt in 1929 after another catastrophic earthquake.

Although in early Christian times Corinth did not flourish in the way in which other Greek cities did, nor was there much significant building activity, as shown by the absence of Byzantine churches, it was one of the first to accept Christianity. One of the most numerous and dynamic of Christian communities

came into being here immediately following Paul's visit, a fact of which he himself felt proud: "I am speaking to you with great frankness, but my pride in you is just as great. In all our many troubles my cup is full of consolation and overflows with joy" (II Cor. 7, 4). There was, however, nothing about the early days of his visit to presage such an outcome. "There he met a Jew named Aquila, a native of Pontus, and his wife Priscilla; they had recently arrived from Italy because Claudius had issued an edict that all Jews should leave Rome. Paul approached them and, because he was of the same trade, he made his home with them; they were tentmakers and Paul worked with them. He also held discussions in the synagogue Sabbath by Sabbath, trying to convince both Jews and Gentiles. Then Silas and Timothy came down from Macedonia, and Paul devoted himself entirely to preaching, maintaining before the Jews that the Messiah is Jesus. When, however, they opposed him and resorted to abuse, he shook out the folds of his cloak and declared, 'Your blood be on your own heads! My conscience is clear! From now on I shall go to the Gentiles. With that he left, and went to the house of a worshipper of God named Titius Justus, who lived next door to the synagogue. Crispus, the president of the synagogue, became a believer in the Lord, as did all his household; and a number of Corinthians who heard him believed and were baptized. One night in a vision the Lord said to Paul, 'Have no fear; go on with your preaching and do not be silenced. I am with you, and no attack shall harm you, for I have many in this city who are my people.' So he settled there for eighteen months, teaching the word of God among them" (Acts 18, 2 - 11).

The first people with whom Paul had to do in Corinth were Aquila and Priscil-

114. Corinth, marble inscription from the main entrance of a Jewish Synagogue

115. Corinth, the Latin inscription of Erastus

la, who, as Jews, had been driven out of Rome. We do not know whether they had already embraced Christianity or whether this happened as a result of their contact with Paul. However this may be, they formed a firm and long-lasting friendship, since apart from their provision of hospitality, they belonged to the same craft. At this point, the narrative of the Acts of the Apostles provides us with an important detail: the work which he proudly engaged in on his journeys, so that he would not be an expense to anyone, was that of tent-making. In all probability, the workshop of Aquila and Priscilla was in the city's Agora, the centre for a great variety of commercial activities.

Another piece of information to be derived from the same passage concerns the return of Silas and Timothy, whom Paul had sent for while he was still in Athens. On their arrival from Thessaloniki they informed him of the news from the church there, whereupon Paul wrote the first Epistle to the Thessalonians and sent it with Timothy. Some weeks later a second epistle was sent to the same church.

At the same time, Paul's teaching in the synagogue of Corinth continued, but did not have the results which he would have wished. Yet again, Paul angered by the Jews, decided to address himself to the Gentiles, hoping that they would be more receptive. Nevertheless, the fact that the president of the synagogue and his household were converted to Christianity could be regarded as a major success. The letters of Paul supply us with the names of a

number of other Corinthians who believed in Christ, apart from Aquila, Priscilla, Crispus and Justus. One of these is of special interest since it has received confirmation from archaeological research. To the north of the Roman forum the following Latin inscription has been found: ERASTUS PRO AEDILITATE S P STRAVIT, which could be translated "Constructed at the expense of Erastus, while he was aedile". In the Epistle to the Romans, written during Paul's third visit in 57/58 AD, there is a clear reference to the same person: "Greetings ... from Erastus, treasurer of this city" (Rom. 16, 23). It would seem, then, that Paul's preaching met with a response even among those who held public office, including the aedile (treasurer), who was responsible chiefly for public buildings and public spectacles.

Paul remained at Corinth for a year and six months, working and preaching. On a number of occasions, however, he was disappointed by the reaction of his audience. Another vision of Christ encouraged him to continue his efforts and not to lose heart in the face of his tribulations. This provided him with the spiritual stamina to endure further persecution. "But when Gallio was proconsul of Achaia, the Jews made a concerted attack on Paul and brought him before the court.

116. Lechaion, the Basilica of St Leonidis, about 460 BC
117. Lechaion, view of the site where the Basilica of St Leonidis was built

'This man', they said, 'is inducing people to worship God in ways that are against the law.' Paul was just about to speak when Gallio declared, 'If it had been about a question of crime or grave misdemeanour, I should, of course, have given you Jews a patient hearing, but if it is some bickering about words and names and your Jewish law, you may settle it yourselves. I do not intend to be a judge of these matters.' And he dismissed them from the court. Then they all attacked Sosthenes, the president of the synagogue, and beat him up in full view of the tribunal. But all this left Gallio quite unconcerned. Paul stayed on at Corinth for some time, and then took leave of the congregation. Accompanied by Priscilla and Aquila, he sailed for Syria, having had his hair cut off at Cenchreae in fulfilment of a vow" (Acts 18, 12 - 18).

Junius Gallio was the son of Lucius Seneca and brother of the famous philosopher Seneca. He had been adopted in Rome by the orator Lucius Junius Gallio, whose name he took. At the time of Paul's visit to Corinth, he was Proconsul of Achaea; in 65 AD he was put to death on the orders of Nero, or, according to another account, committed suicide. The attitude which he adopted in the face of the accusations of the Jews against Paul was one of moderation and in line with the approach of many Roman officials, who preferred not to involve themselves in the religious disputes of the Jews. The site of Gallio's judgment seat has been identified with the 'Bema' (rostrum) of the Roman

forum of Corinth, to the south of its 'piazza', among numerous shops. Today, remains of the Bema are to be found under the foundations of a small church built on the spot in the tenth century.

Paul left Corinth by the port of Cenchreae, near the present-day village of Kechries. There he cut his hair as an offering to God, in accordance with a Jewish custom. At Cenchreae a Christian community grew up at an early date, with a woman named Phoebe as its deaconess ('minister'): "I commend to you Phoebe, a fellow-Christian who is a minister in the church at Cenchreae. Give her, in the fellowship of the Lord, a welcome worthy of God's people, and support her in any business in which she may need your help, for she has herself been a good friend to many, including myself" (Rom. 16, 1 - 2). Archaeological investigations in the area have brought to light parts of the harbour and its buildings, most of which are now below sea level. Close to the harbour the remains of a small early Christian basilica, built on the site of a Roman sanctuary of Isis, have been found.

During the course of his third journey, while he was at Ephesus in 55 AD, Paul was informed that the church at Corinth was troubled by various problems and disputes. As a result, he sent with Timothy his First Epistle to the Corinthians, reproving them for their unruly conduct and setting down his views on various is-

119. Cenchreae, part of the ancient harbour with the remains of an early Christian Basilica

sues of Christian ethics. A little later, he visited Corinth for a second time, in order to follow the situation in person, although he had in the meantime received further news from Timothy. After this brief visit he returned to Ephesus and then set out to the cities of Macedonia. While he was at Philippi, he received news from Titus that the problems of the Corinthians were beginning to be solved, whereupon he sent them his Second Epistle, urging them to make a collection for the church of Jerusalem. Later, when a considerable sum had also been collected in Macedonia, he made a third visit to Corinth in 57/58 AD. He had decided to return to Syria by ship, but when he learnt that certain Jews had plotted to kill him, he decided to return by land through Macedonia.

In the present-day city of Corinth there is a church dedicated to the Apostle Paul, consecrated by the Metropolitan Damaskinos in 1934 (Aghiou Pavlou St). Opposite this church there is a museum of church art with very interesting exhibits.

THE END OF THE SECOND JOURNEY

Leaving the port of Cenchreae, Paul crossed the Aegean Sea and landed at Ephesus in Asia Minor. Leaving Aquila and Priscilla there, he went on to Caesarea and passing through Jerusalem, reached Antioch. This was his last visit to Antioch, the city which the starting-point for his missionary journeys.

120-121. (above)
Corinth, the Acrocorinth,
the acropolis of the
ancient and medieval
town

120. (below) Corinth,
view of the Acrocorinth

121. (below) Corinth,
the Church of Apostle
Paul in the modern town

THIRD JOURNEY

aul's third journey began from Antioch in 52 AD and must have been completed in 58. The first cities in which he taught were those of Galatia and Phrygia. It seems that while in those parts he fell seriously ill, though the nature of his illness is not known to us. " ... It was bodily illness, as you will remember, that originally led to my bringing you the gospel, and you resisted any temptation to show scorn or disgust at my physical condition; on the contrary you welcomed me as if I were an angel of God, as you might have welcomed Christ Jesus himself" (Gal. 4, 13 - 14).

When he was out of danger, he continued to Ephesus, where he was imprisoned. From there he sent his first letter to the Corinthians and, in all probability, paid a brief visit to their city. On his return to Ephesus, he wrote the Epistle to the Galatians. He then travelled in Macedonia, writing his Second Epistle to the Corinthians from Philippi, a little before visiting their city for a third time. During the course of his three-month stay in Corinth, he wrote the Epistle to the Romans, which was dispatched from the port of Cenchreae, while he himself prepared to leave by sea. However, Jewish plots against his life forced him to return through Macedonia. Thus he travelled by land to Neapolis, took ship to the Troad and went on to Assos.

122. Byzantine capital

123. Ephesus, view of the archaeological site. In the background: the Library of Celsus (left)

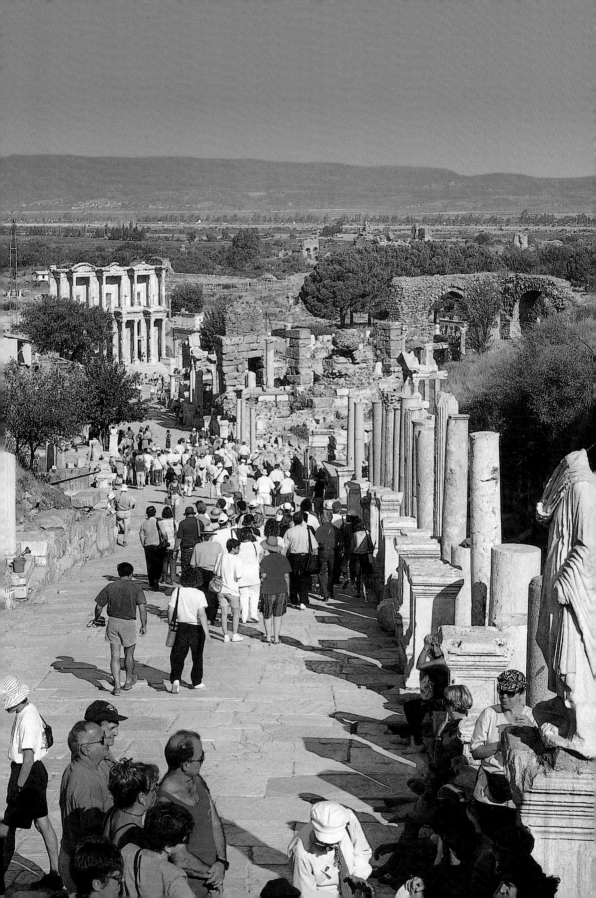

MYTILENE
CHIOS - SAMOS

*"We went on ahead to the ship and embarked for Assos, where we were to take
Paul aboard; this was the arrangement he had made, since he was going to travel
by road. When he met us at Assos, we took him aboard and proceeded to Mytilene.
We sailed from there and next day arrived off Chios. On the second day we made
Samos, and the following day we reached Miletus" (Acts 20, 13 - 15).*

As can be seen from the above passage, Luke met up with Paul and his companions and was with him when he visited Mytilene, Chios and Samos. Apart from the fact that their stay lasted three days in all, we know nothing of their visit to these islands. Nonetheless, tradition claims that Paul's vessel, on arrival at Mytilene (Lesbos - the modern Lesvos), put in at the Bay of Kalloni, in the south, where, on a beach in the village of Vasilika, a chapel has been built to honour him.

124. Mytilene, view from the village of Molyvos - 125. Mytilene, the Church of St Therapon, 1860

Mytilene or Lesvos is Greece's third largest island and lies in the north-eastern Aegean, close to the Asia Minor coast. Its first inhabitants established themselves in the region of Thermi in the fourth millennium BC and are probably to be associated with the settler Makaras, whose name occurs in the mythological tradition. In the course of the second millennium it was inhabited successively by the Pelasgians, the Achaeans, and finally by the Aeolians, who dominated the whole island, built up their maritime power and founded colonies in Thrace and Asia Minor. In the seventh and sixth centuries BC, Lesbos was in the forefront of Greek culture in its encouragement of the arts and literature. It was the birthplace of Pittacus, one of the Seven Sages of antiquity, as well as of the poets Alcaeus, Sappho, Terpander and Arion, who laid the foundations of lyrical poetry. Between 492 and 479 BC it was under Persian rule, and subsequently allied itself with the Athenians. In 428 BC it was punished severely for its apostasy from the Athenian Alliance and its land was divided up among Athenian settlers. The islanders took an active part in Alexander the Great's campaign. After his death, they came under the rule of the Ptolemies and then of the Romans (88 BC). In the Byzantine period, the island was a province of the Empire until 1355, when it was given as a dowry to the Genoese Francesco Gattelusio. It subsequently developed into an important commercial and economic centre for the northern Aegean. Today, the green and picturesque island of Mytilene has a wide variety of at-tractions for visitors. In the area of its capital, Mytilene (from which the whole island takes its alternative name), of particular note are the Byzantine fortress with its Venetian additions, the nineteenth-century mansions, the ancient theatre of the Hellenistic period, the modern church, renowned for its miracles, of St Raphael at Thermi, and the museum of the works of the naif painter Theofilos at Vareia. In the rest of the island there are its attractive fishing-villages, the town of Molyvos with the fortress of the Gattelusi, Ayiasos with its Church of Our Lady, and Sigri with its petrified forest millions of years old.

The rocky island of Chios, not far to the south of Mytilene, is different in character. Known as Makris and Ophiousa in antiquity, its first recorded inhabitants were Leleges and Pelasgians, while in historical times it was colonised by Ionians from Attica. In the Classical period, after a period of Persian occupation (499 - 479 BC), it became an ally of Athens, but soon tired of the latter's domination. In 355 BC, after many years of conflict with the Athenians, the people of Chios recovered their independence. The island was taken by the Macedonians in 331 BC; in 84 BC it was declared by the Romans a free ally of the Empire, but a few years after Paul's visit it lost its independence and formed a part of the Roman province of the Greek islands (70 AD). During the Byzantine period, Chios endured, for many centuries, raids carried out by Saracen pirates (seventh to eleventh centuries); in the eleventh century it equipped itself with strong fortifications. From that

point on, its importance grew and it became the capital of a Byzantine theme (administrative region) of the same name. It was during this period that the island's most important Byzantine monument was built: the Nea Moni ('New Monastery'). Its katholikon (main church) was constructed at the expense of the Emperor Constantine Monomachus in the octagonal architectural style and was adorned with mosaics of outstanding quality.

In 1346, Chios passed into the hands of the Genoese and remained under their rule until 1566, when it was taken by the Turks. Under Genoese rule, the so-called 'mastic villages' in the south of the island grew up. These medieval villages, with their fortifications, almost the sole source of mastic gum, are still very much alive, and provide a unique insight into the architecture of that period. Their production of mastic was the reason for their acquisition of privileges under Turkish rule and for the development of trade and industry. In 1822, in the course of the War of Independence, the population of Chios were subjected to appalling massacres at the hands of the Turks. Their final liberation came in 1912.

South of Chios lies Samos, an island which throughout its history has been one of the most important centres of political and cultural developments. Its south-eastern coast, in the area where the city of Samos was to grow up in historical times, was inhabited for the first time in the fourth millennium BC. The Hellenes came to dominate the area in the second millennium, after they had driven out the Carians and Leleges. Around 900 BC the first Ionian colonists, who were responsible for the island's subsequent development, established themselves. As early as the ninth and eighth centuries BC great progress was made in the field of art, with the Samians combining the trends prevalent in Attica and in the Greek cities of Asia Minor. Its earliest temple to Hera, the island's presiding deity, who had been worshipped in a permanent sanctuary (Heraion) since the tenth century, was built in the eighth or seventh century BC. A number of other temples dedicated to Hera were built down to the sixth century, those of Rhoecus and Theodorus (570 - 560 BC) and that of Polycrates (c. 525 BC) being of major importance. Rhoecus and Theodorus were two pioneering architects and workers in bronze whose temple of Hera contributed to the evolution of the Ionic order of architecture, while Polycrates was tyrant of the island from 532 to 522 BC. His temple to Hera was the largest temple in Greece, an attempt to advertise his power and wealth. His reign saw the construction of fine public works and the high point of the island's prosperity. Pythogoras, the philosopher and mathematician, was born here in the sixth century BC, a fact commemorated in the name of the village of Pythagoreio. Until it was conquered by the Romans in 131 BC, Samos was dependent upon the Persians and on the policies of Athens, Sparta and the Macedonian kings. In Byzantine times it was raided by the Goths, Huns, Alani, and Saracen pirates and passed through the hands of the Latins and the Genoese. After the fall of Constantinople in 1453, it was laid waste, and it was only after 1562, still under Turkish rule, that it started to be resettled. It achieved autonomy in 1832 and union with Greece in 1912.

127. Chios, windmills at a port of the island
128. Samos, view from the village Pythagoreio
129. Samos, the unique reconstructed column from the Temple of Hera built by tyrant Polycrates in the Sanctuary of Hera (Heraion), about 525 BC

COS - RHODES

fter his visit to Samos, Paul disembarked at Miletus and, having been informed of the state of affairs in Ephesus by his envoys, sailed for Cos and Rhodes (Acts 21, 1).

Cos, which today belongs to the Dodecanese group of islands, lies in the southern Aegean, close to the Asia Minor coast. The first settlers on the island were Pelasgians; these were followed by the Achaeans and Dorians, who, having dominated the region in the seventh century BC, formed an alliance of six cities, the Hexapolis, which included Cos. After the Persian Wars, it became a member of the Delian League, and in the Peloponnesian War fought on the side of Athens. In the mid fifth century BC, Hippocrates, the famous physician and descendant, according to tradition, of the divine healer Asclepius, was born on Cos. Asclepius was worshipped from a very early date on the island; in the fourth century a sanctuary dedicated to him, which enjoyed great renown in the two centuries which followed, began to operate. Here patients were said to be cured in their sleep, after invoking the aid of Asclepius. In Hellenistic times, Cos was one of the strongest maritime powers in the eastern Mediterranean. In 82 BC it was taken by the Romans and its decline began. In Byzantine times it was raided by the Slavs, the Bulgars, Saracen pirates, the Genoese, the Venetians, and the Knights of St John. It fell into the hands of the Turks in 1522 and into those of the Italians in 1912. It was finally incorporated into the Greek state in 1948.

According to local tradition, Paul preached in the city of Cos beneath the so-called plane tree of Hippocrates, where the great physician of antiquity also taught. In a similar way, the people of Rhodes hold that Paul entered their city by the gate in the wall which today bears his name and that he then visited Lindos, in the south of the island. At Lindos there had been since the Archaic period a temple dedicated to Athena Lindia, which was replaced by a new Doric temple around 330 BC. In the second century BC the sanctuary of Athena, the highest point of the acropolis of Lindos, was adorned with new buildings and became the island's most important re-

ligious centre. At the little harbour below the acropolis of Lindos, named after St Paul, there is a small church commemorating his visit.

Rhodes is the capital and largest island of the Dodecanese. It was inhabited in prehistoric times and with the passage of the centuries became one of the most important commercial centres in the Mediterranean. In the sixth century BC, Lindos in particular flourished under the tyrant Cleobulus -another of the Seven Sages of the ancient world. In 408 BC the three major Dorian cities of Kameiros, Ialysos and Lindos united to form a single city. This was called Rhodes and soon became very prosperous.

In 305/4 BC, the Rodians successfully resisted the siege of the Macedonian Demetrius Poliorcetes and used the spoils of victory to construct the Colossus, one of the Seven Wonders of the World- a statue 30 metres high, the work of the sculptor Chares of Lindos. From the second century BC the fate of Rhodes was linked with that of Rome, but in 42 BC it was laid waste by Cassius, who took precious works of art belonging to the island to Rome. During the Byzantine period, Rhodes was the object of raiding and looting, particularly by the Arabs, while in 1309 it passed into the hands of the Knights of the Order of St John, who graced it with magnificent buildings, many of which still stand today. Rhodes was taken by the Turks in 1522 and passed to the Italians in 1912. Union with Greece came in 1948.

131. (above) Cos, the Temple of Apollo (2nd cantury AD) at the Sanctuary of Asclepius (Asclepeion)

131. (below left) Cos, reconstructed Odeon in the town of Cos, 2nd century AD

131. (below right) Cos, the so-called plane tree of Hippocrates, under which, according to tradition, Paul preached

132-133. (above) Rhodes, a little harbour below the acropolis of Lindos, named after St Paul in memory of his visit

132-133. (below) Rhodes, view of Lindos. In the background: the acropolis of Lindos

CRETE

❧

From the harbour of Rhodes, Paul went on to the coast of Asia Minor, and from there continued by sea to Tyre in Syria. He then travelled to Jerusalem via Ptolemais and Caesarea. In Jerusalem the Jews attempted to murder him, but the Roman commandant arrested him and allowed him to speak in his own defence. After the discovery of the Jewish plot against him, Paul made his escape to Caesarea, where, after he had made his defence before the Roman authorities of the region and Herod Agrippa, King of Syria, it was decided that he should go to Rome. This journey was made by sea, with Sidon and Myra in Lycia as the first stopping-places. Because of adverse weather conditions, a change of course became necessary, bringing Paul to the south coast of Crete.

Crete, Greece's largest island, was in mythology the birthplace of Zeus, the most senior of the gods of Olympus. Inhabited since the Neolithic period, the island came to dominate the Mediterranean in the Bronze Age and produced the first European civilisation, Minoan culture. According to the mythological tradition, Minoan domination of the sea was due to the island's wise lawgiver and king, Minos. Excavations at the palaces of Knossos, Phaistos, Malia and Zakros, as well as of large numbers of luxury villas and commercial and manufacturing premises, have confirmed the existence of a highly-developed civilisation and a well-organised state. Moreover, the finds, to be found today in the island's museums, are irrefutable evidence of the high standard of living of the Minoans and of their artistic abilities. The Minoan palaces were destroyed twice: in 1700 BC and in 1450 - 1380 BC. The second destruction marked the point when the ascendancy of Crete gave way to the constantly increasing power of the Mycenaeans of the mainland. Between 1100 and 900 BC, new settlers, Dorians and Achaeans, arrived and the old cities were abandoned. Nevertheless, by the sixth century BC the inhabitants had succeeded in making new progress in commerce and the arts, and the island was serving as a bridge between Greece and the East. During the Classical period, Crete was cut off from the other Greek city-states and there was considerable internal upheaval on the island, which continued into Hellenistic times. In 69 BC, Crete was taken by the Romans, who brought to the island a period of peace and prosperity. In the second century AD, the Emperor Hadrian showed the island particular favour and adorned its cities with fine buildings. In 824 AD, Crete was detached from the Byzantine Empire by the Saracens, but was liberated by Nicephorus Phocas in 961. After 1204 it was sold to the Venetians, to be conquered by the Turks in 1669. In 1898, the island was declared independent and was united to Greece in 1913. In the Second World War it was the scene of the famous Battle of Crete and of heroic resistance against the Nazis.

Crete today is one the most popular of Greece's islands with visitors. This fact is to explained by the wealth of its history, in harmonious conjunction with its natural beauty. The blue seas and the mountain villages in the traditional style, the colours of the olive and the vine, the sound of the Cretan lyre and the hospitable friendliness of the Cretans give the island a character which is unique. In Crete, summer lasts a good deal longer than the three months which it is elsewhere and sunny days account for the greater part of the year. On the other hand, the heat is cooled, even in summer, by the 'meltemi', a wind which often reaches gale force, particularly in the south of the island. It seems that Paul's vessel encountered exactly this kind

of bad weather as it approached the coast of Crete, rendering it necessary for it to anchor on this coast, in the area of Kaloi Limenes.

" ... We began to sail under the lee of Crete, and, hugging the coast, struggled on to a place called Fair Havens, not far from the town of Lasea. By now much time had been lost, and with the Fast already over, it was dangerous to go on with the voyage. So Paul gave them this warning: 'I can see, gentlemen, that this voyage will be disastrous: it will mean heavy loss, not only of ship and cargo but also of life.' But the centurion paid more attention to the captain and to the owner of the ship than to what Paul said; and as the harbour was unsuitable for wintering, the majority were in favour of putting to sea, hoping, if they could get so far, to winter at Phoenix, a Cretan harbour facing south-west and north-west. When a southerly breeze sprang up, they thought that their purpose was as good as achieved, and, weighing anchor, they sailed along the coast of Crete hugging the land. But before very long a violent wind, the Northeaster as they call it, swept down from the landward side. It caught the ship and, as it was impossible to keep head to the wind, we

134. Crete, view of the Minoan Palace of Cnossos

136. Crete, the village of Loutro, which is identified with Phoenix, the Cretan harbour referred in the "Acts of the Apostles"

137. Crete, the small Church of Apostle Paul near Loutro

had to give way and run before it" (Acts 27, 8 - 15).

According to the prevailing view, Paul's voyage to Kaloi Limenes ('Fair Havens') must have taken place in the autumn of 61 AD. Kaloi Limenes is at Crete's southernmost point, close to the ancient city of Gortyn and its port, Lebena. The town of Lasea referred to in Acts was east of Lebena, while 'Phoenix' should probably be identified with what is today the village of Loutro, in the Prefecture of Chania. Although we are not told this in the written sources, local tradition maintains that Paul visited Loutro, as well as Kaloi Limenes. Very near the village there is a chapel dedicated to St Paul, of a date earlier than the fifteenth century, just as there is a small church at Kaloi Limenes commemorating his visit, while a nearby cave, marked by a wooden cross, is held to be where he stayed.

We do not know how long Paul's ship stayed at Kaloi Limenes before the decision to carry on to Phoenix was taken, or what results this visit had. However, most scholars believe that Paul paid another visit to Crete, after his release from detention in 64 AD. This view is based on a passage in the Epistle to Titus and is disputed chiefly by those who question its Pauline authorship: "My intention in leaving you behind in Crete was that you should deal with any outstanding matters, and in particular should appoint elders in each town in accordance with the principles which I have laid down" (Titus 1, 5). It is to be concluded from this that Paul travelled to

Crete and left Titus behind him. It would seem that Paul was somewhat anxious about the Christians of Crete, since, as he wrote in his epistle: "It was a Cretan prophet, one of their own countrymen, who said, 'Cretans were ever liars, vicious brutes, lazy gluttons' - and how truly he spoke! All the more reason why you should rebuke them sharply, so that they may be restored to a sound faith" (Titus, 1, 12 - 13). The quotation which Paul us-

es is attributed to the poet, legislator and seer Epimenides, who was born in the seventh century BC at Knossos.

In spite of this, Crete was one of the first regions of the Greek world to accept Christianity, since a Christian community was quickly formed, with Titus as their bishop. After his death, Titus became patron saint of the island and his feast day is observed on 25 August. At Gortyn, the capital of the island under Roman rule, a basilica dedicated to St Titus was built in the seventh century. This was rebuilt in the tenth century and today retains its eastern three-sided apse in good condition. There is also a church dedicated to St Titus in Irakleio; in the Byzantine period this was the city's cathedral.

138-139. Crete, the Church of St Titus in Gortys, 7th century AD

THE END
OF PAUL

The stormy wind - a familiar feature of the eastern Mediterranean in summer and autumn - carried Paul's vessel into the Adriatic and cast it up on the rocks, but all the passengers landed safely on Melita (Malta). There Paul was attacked by a viper, but with God's help escaped danger. From Malta, a fresh ship took Paul, by way of Syracuse, Rhegium and Puteoli to Rome, where he was under house arrest for two years, but at liberty to be visited by the local Christians and to teach (62 - 64 AD). During the course of this first detention, Paul wrote his letters to the Philippians, Colossians, Philemon, and the Ephesians, though some believe that some of these were written when he was detained at Ephesus. For a time Paul was at liberty and, according to tradition, was able to make a fourth journey which included Spain, Asia Minor, Crete, Macedonia, and Illyria. This would seem to be the period at which the First and Second Epistles to Timothy and the Epistle to Titus were written. On his return to Rome, Paul was imprisoned for a second time and in 67 AD died a martyr's death during the persecutions of Nero.

The death sentence passed on Paul robbed humanity of perhaps the greatest ambassador of Christianity the world has seen, but it was not able to shake the founda-

140. Byzantine coin

141. Crete, Apostle Paul, mosaic from the Church of Apostle Paul in the modern town of Corinth

tions of his work. His efforts had already born fruit while he was alive, since Christian communities were founded one after the other following each visit to the cities of the Mediterranean. His ardent preaching and his constant care for the organisation of the churches provided the Christians with a necessary support for the strengthening of their faith. The principles which Paul passionately taught served as an inexhaustible source of strength for persecuted Christians, especially under Nero and Diocletian. Thus the message of Christianity, in spite of merciless persecution, succeeded in spreading throughout the Roman state, gaining ever-increasing numbers of followers, until in the time of Constantine (305 - 337 AD) it touched the heart of the Emperor himself. In 381 AD, thanks to the decrees of Theodosius (379 - 395 AD), it became the official religion of the state. In the course of the four centuries which were needed for the message of Jesus Christ to become established there were many who strove and bore witness even to the point of death, remaining firm in their faith and thus setting an example to every Christian. Among them, the figure of Paul sums up all the strivings of Christians, while his work as a missionary is the culmination of them. Rightly is he regarded today as, after Christ Himself, the second founder of the Christian religion.

142. The Descent of Christ to Hades (the Resurrection), mosaic from the Monastery of Hosios (Blessed) Lukas, about 1030-1040 AD